D1269260

SOTSGOROD

THE MIT PRESS CAMBRIDGE, MASSACHUSETTS, AND LONDON, ENGLAND

SOTSGOROD

THE PROBLEM OF BUILDING SOCIALIST CITIES

N. A. MILIUTIN

TRANSLATED FROM THE RUSSIAN BY
ARTHUR SPRAGUE (1931–1968)

PREPARED FOR PUBLICATION BY
GEORGE R. COLLINS AND WILLIAM ALEX

NA
9211
.M5413

Miliutin, N. A.

Sotsgorod

309.26 M64

Copyright © 1974 by
The Massachusetts Institute of Technology

This book was designed by The MIT Press Design
Department.
It was set in CRT Futura
by The Colonial Press Inc.
printed on Mead Moistrite Matte
by Halliday Lithograph Corp.
and bound in G.S.B. S/535/9 Black
by The Colonial Press Inc.
in the United States of America.

Sotsgorod was originally published in 1930 by
the State Publishing House RSFSR. All rights
reserved. No part of this book may be reproduced in any form or by any means, electronic
or mechanical, including photocopying, record-
ing, or by any information storage and retrieval
system, without permission in writing from the
publisher.

Library of Congress Cataloging in Publication
Data

Miliutin, Nikolaĭ Aleksandrovich, 1889–1942
    Sotsgorod; the problem of building socialist
cities.

    Translation of Sotsgorod.
    1. Constructivism (Architecture)—Russia.
2. Cities and towns—Planning—Russia.
I. Collins, George R. II. Title.
NA9211.M5413   309.2′62′0947   72–13429
ISBN 0–262–13089–0

DABNEY LANCASTER LIBRARY
LONGWOOD COLLEGE
FARMVILLE, VIRGINIA 23901

CONTENTS

76-04556

PREFACE

Shortly after Arthur Sprague's death in 1968, his friends and academic associates at Columbia University decided that at least a portion of the work in which he had been engaged should be made available through publication. This work was primarily in the field of Russian architecture and town planning between the two World Wars, which is perhaps the aspect of the modern movement that is least accessible to western scholars; Arthur Sprague's contribution to our understanding of this period would have been considerable. He had almost finished the draft of his doctoral dissertation on Soviet Constructivist Architecture 1917–34, working on it as a Fellow of Columbia's Russian Institute, when, in the early summer of 1968, he was killed in an automobile accident.

Sprague had earned his M.A. at Columbia in 1967 with a thesis on N. A. Miliutin and Linear Planning in the USSR and had earlier prepared in connection with his work on that subject the translation of Miliutin's book which forms the core of the present volume.

He received his A.B. from Columbia College in 1953 and then began graduate studies at the University's Department of Slavic Languages under the guidance of Rufus W. Mathewson, Jr.; later he became a doctoral candidate in the Department of Art History and Archaeology, working mainly with Professor George Collins. He was fluent in Russian and spent a year and a half at Moscow State University as an exchange student and Fellow of the Inter-University Committee on Travel Grants. He also received grants and fellowships from the Ford Foundation and the American Council of Learned Societies, among others. During the period 1964–67, as an Assistant Professor at Waynesburg College, he taught courses in modern art and architecture and studio painting: he was active as a painter and had devoted a year to that interest in Mexico during the 1950s.

Before his career ended he began a series of articles that showed great promise. He wrote "Chernikhov and Constructivism," for the London *Survey* (Winter, 1961); he furnished a number of entries, including those on Russian and Soviet Architecture, for the *Encyclopedia of Modern Architecture* (Abrams, 1964); he contributed the chapter "Modernizing Architecture, Art and Town Plans in Soviet Central Asia," in *Central Asia: A Century of Russian Rule* (Edward Allworth, Editor, Columbia University Press, 1967). And he wrote book reviews for the *Slavic Review.* He was also preparing a portfolio of architectural drawings of the work of the Russian architect Konstantin Melnikov (a project that has been taken over for completion by Professor S. Frederick Starr of Princeton University).

The original draft translation of Miliutin's *Sotsgorod* has been carefully corrected and refined with the assistance of Tanya Page of Columbia's Department of Slavic Languages. The search for exactness of meaning and the most appropriate English equivalents were often the subject of long consideration before Miss Page, an accomplished linguist, would be satisfied.

Miliutin's prose is not easy to translate. It appears to have been written hastily with little polishing, so that it is somewhat loose, rambling, and repetitive in places. It is inflated with the rhetoric of the times, and some words obviously carried special contemporary meanings that are now lost to us. Also, Miliutin tends to marshal his arguments in numbered sequences that give a misleading appearance of order to the points he makes. The numbered categories are not always of a correspondence or symmetry and are not always of the same weight and importance. The result is sometimes difficult to follow so far as logic is concerned, but the effect—the enthusiasm—is perhaps the more human for this, and, in the end, more convincing. His use of bold-face type for emphasis also seems erratic at times, but we have followed him scrupulously in this respect. However, we have not carried over the letterspacing common to Russian typography.

Some of his quotations from non-Russian Marxist authors vary somewhat from the accepted English versions. In all cases we have translated the quotations as Miliutin printed them and have added a note if our understanding of the passage is different.

The design of the book is, of course,

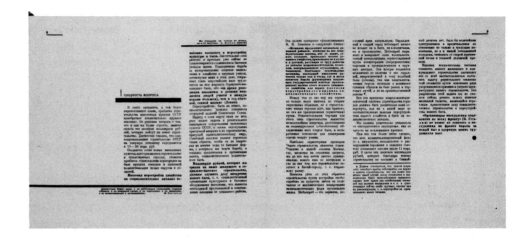

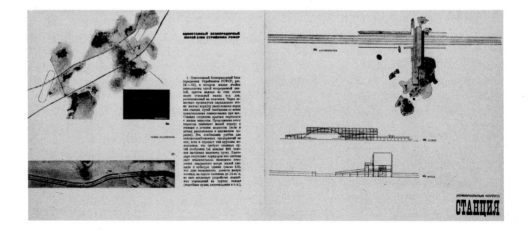

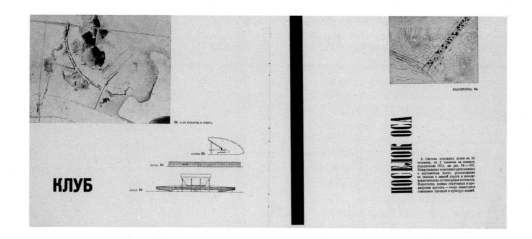

one of its strengths. It was published at the very peak of Constructivist-Suprematist enthusiasm at the Government Printing Office in Moscow. Many of its page-layouts are as striking as posters by El Lissitzky or as pages in the avant-garde magazine *SA*. Unfortunately the quality of reproduction of pictures was not up to the graphic design. They are rather grey in the original; Boris Martens, who reviewed and summarized the book in 1932, already complained about this.

In setting up the translated text we have tried to adhere to the original placement and design so that our translation achieves a facsimile effect as closely as possible. We lose, of course, the rectangular effect of the original Russian letters, as can be seen by comparing the pages of the present translation to those pages of the original that we have reproduced in this Preface.

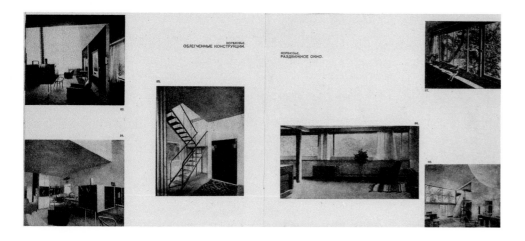

The responsibilities of the undersigned for the present volume were roughly as follows: George Collins worked with Miss Page on the reviewing of the translation and also assembled the various supporting materials—the notes to the translation, the Introduction and its notes, the Glossary, Bibliography, plates, etc. William Alex, a close friend of Arthur Sprague, participated in the original planning of the publication, in the final stages of the translation work with Miss Page, and in general matters of design.

In composing the Introduction, the intention has been to incorporate as much as possible of Arthur Sprague's M.A. essay on

Miliutin. The following passages in the Introduction have been taken more or less bodily from that essay: Soviet planning prior to 1930; details of Ginzburg and his Domnarkomfin building; Miliutin's biography; Fordization in the USSR; most of the data about Magnitogorsk, Stalingrad, and Avtostroi; the circumstances of Miliutin's recantation and the content of his later publications in *Sovetskaia Arkhitektura*; most of the four concluding paragraphs. The materials in this volume not specifically listed as Sprague's here or on pp. 35, 129 were contributed by George Collins, who wrote the Introduction in its final form and edited the entire book.

We have been very much assisted by the numerous publications in the field that have appeared since the present translation was started in the early 1960s, in particular Anatole Kopp's *Town and Revolution*, the new augmented MIT Press edition of El Lissitzky's *Russland*, and Paolo Ceccarelli's recent collection of documents of the period. This indebtedness is made clear throughout our notes. We have added about 30 items to the Bibliography as it appeared in Arthur Sprague's M.A. essay, and eliminated about a dozen of his citations that were sufficiently listed in one or another of his notes. Our General Bibliography is not intended to be a comprehensive listing for the field of Soviet architecture and urbanism. Rather, it contains titles of works used by Arthur Sprague and ourselves in translating and situating Miliutin's book.

We are grateful for the direct assistance in this project of Professor Edward Allworth of Columbia University, Professor S. Frederick Starr of Princeton University, and the reference staff of the Columbia University Library, in particular Eugene P. Sheehy, Rita G. Keckeissen, and Nancy E. Schroeder. We were assisted in the final stages of preparation for publication by the Collins sons—David in translating, Nicolas in proofreading, and Lucas in proofreading and photography. Yael Harussi also helped with translating.

We wish to thank for permission to quote from their works, as cited, the following: the *New York Times*, Random House Inc., Simon & Schuster Inc., Paul L. Willen. We are indebted to the Library of the University of Chicago for lending us its copy of Miliutin's Russian original several times in the course of preparation of this book.

GEORGE R. COLLINS
WILLIAM ALEX
NEW YORK CITY, 1974

INTRODUCTION

N. A. Miliutin's often cited but seldom consulted *Sotsgorod* is a landmark in the history of city planning. Written by a Soviet functionary at the height of controversy in the USSR about the direction in which socialist planning should go, it represents a unique effort to draft a physical plan that is the embodiment of a modern social, political, and industrial creed.

N. A. Miliutin's model plan for a Stalingrad tractor plant (Fig. 14 of the 94 illustrations and diagrams in his book; see p. 71 of this volume) has been illustrated on countless occasions as one of the major theoretical industrial plans of our century. It has been recognized as the source of Le Corbusier's *cité linéaire industrielle* of the 1940s (Pl. 1), and it is clearly the transitional step between Tony Garnier's *cité industrielle* of c. 1900 (Pl. 2) and the codified planning principles of the Athens Charter that were worked out by members of the CIAM when they were dis-invited to meet in Moscow in 1932–33.

Unfortunately, Miliutin's plan has usually been illustrated out of its context and meaning; it has frequently been misdated and misinterpreted; and virtually none of those who write about it have ever taken the trouble to look at, much less to read, the book in which it appeared. The result is that neither its social nor its architectural meaning has been understood; that is to say, the fact has passed unnoticed that it was one of Miliutin's several paradigms of a socio-economic theory of planning by which society itself could be totally transformed. This oversight occurs not merely because of the difficulty of the language, Russian, in which Miliutin wrote: the book, although printed in an edition of 7,000 copies, seems to be quite rare outside of the Soviet Union—which is the major reason that we have decided to translate it.

The paradox of a general familiarity with Miliutin's model plan and yet an ignorance of his text may arise from the rapidly changing political circumstances in the USSR at the time of the appearance of his book. It was printed late in the year 1930 at the very peak of agitated discussion and publication about planning, housing, and the new architecture by Soviet theoreticians. Dispute raged over the most efficacious ways to design minimal residential quarters, communal housing, and collectivized services and as to whether centralization (i.e., urbanization) or decentralization would better serve to achieve that transformation of the way of life demanded by Marxist theory and, in particular, by the Bolshevik Party Congress of May 1930. The fever of the First Five-Year Plan was upon everyone, and orthodox Communists like Miliutin were straining to demonstrate how to apply the rare utterances of Marx, Engels, and Lenin about physical planning to the professional architectural problems of the moment.[1]

Le Corbusier had just been in the Soviet Union,[2] and teams of engineers and architects of several nationalities—especially German and American—were busily engaged at widespread sites throughout the USSR in laying out the separate units of a great power and industrial network. The door to the West was, for the moment, ajar; it was in the summer of 1930 that Margaret Bourke-White was allowed to compile her remarkable photographic record of the frenetic Five-Year Plan activities at many of the sites.[3]

Miliutin's book was known to Russian-speaking members of the foreign colony; it figures in their later recollections of the events, and some of them brought copies out of Russia.[4] This is apparently how his Fig. 14 to which we have referred got into the mainstream of modern city planning. The book fell afoul of Party leadership, however, in the kaleidoscopic shifting of Bolshevik politics, and it may be that its circulation was discouraged or even suppressed a few months after its appearance.

In the polemics of the moment Miliutin occupied a middle ground, and he attempted to mediate between the extreme positions by urging a forward-looking architecture and planning that was at the same time "realistic," i.e., one that took into account the shortcomings of Russia's industrial system during the "transitional" period in her development. This should have earned him the party's plaudits. He had studied intensely and enthusiastically the new Western architecture, especially that of Le Corbusier and of the Bauhaus architects

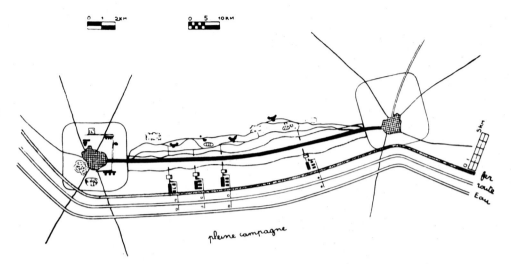

1. LE CORBUSIER. CITÉ LINÉAIRE INDUSTRIELLE, 1942. REPRINTED FROM LE CORBUSIER, *OEUVRES COMPLETES*, VOL. IV, 1938–1946, (ZURICH: GIRSBERGER; 2ND ED., 1950), P. 73.

[Pl. nos. refer to Illustrations in our Introduction. We call Miliutin's illustrations Figs., as he did.—G.R.C.]

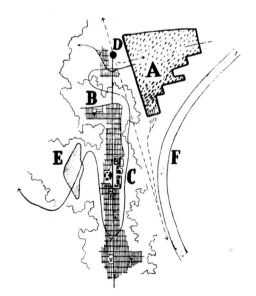

2. TONY GARNIER. CITE INDUSTRIELLE, C. 1900. A, INDUSTRY: B, RESIDENTIAL ZONE WITH AXIAL BOULEVARD: C, CIVIC CENTER: D, RAILROAD STATION AND HISTORIC TOWN CENTER; E, HOSPITAL ZONE: F, RIVER. REPRINTED FROM C. B. PURDOM, *THE BUILDING OF SATELLITE TOWNS*, (LONDON: DENT, 1949), P. 13.

(Gropius, Mies van der Rohe, Hannes Meyer), and he was venomous in his comments about the old-line academicians still practicing in the Soviet Union. This may have done him disservice in the days to come. But what actually tripped him up was his expansive use in the book of a number of drawings from his friend Moisei Ginzburg's latest project "Green City" which proposed the decentralization of large urban centers, in this case Moscow. At the next Bolshevik Party Congress (that of June 1931, which signaled the conclusion of the period of excited theorizing that we have described), the decentralists and visionaries were roundly condemned, and Lazar Kaganovich singled out Miliutin especially for having suggested that Moscow be dispersed—a position that Miliutin had not explicitly taken in the book. Miliutin nevertheless recanted, as we shall see, and the fact that he wrote *Sotsgorod* is nowhere mentioned in his official Soviet biographies. This is the more ironic because of his enthusiastic use in argumentation of statistical data from bona fide Soviet sources and his considerable criticism of the plans drawn up by certain of the foreign teams then operating in Russia and of some of the more radical collectivist schemes by Russian architects.

In any case, his little-known text deserves to be read in full, if only to savor the way in which it expresses the boundless optimism of its moment and place in world history,[5] but more particularly so that Miliutin's famous linear industrial plan can be understood for all the social and economic ratiocination that lies behind it. That simple diagram is as loaded with symbolism and the fervor of the moment as is the frontispiece of a great Carolingian bible, and only through a careful perusal of the text and times can the meaning of either become clear.

As an introduction to Miliutin's text, we would like to deal with the following:

The state of Soviet town planning before the late 1920s, and some of the individuals and organizations that were involved with Miliutin during the period of the First Five-Year Plan. Biographical data about him. The major points that he stressed in his writing and some possible sources for his ideas. An analysis of his book by chapters. His later writings about planning and their relation to the deepening crisis in Soviet ideology. Some speculations about his influence, then and now.

The State of Soviet Town Planning before 1930

Due to the scarcity of material on Soviet planning of the 1920s that is available to readers unfamiliar with the Russian language, a considerable survey is offered here of the major events of early Soviet planning.[6] This is in no way intended to be a complete, or even an entirely systematic, outline of early Soviet developments, but rather a setting of the stage for Miliutin's theory; it is meant to illustrate the limited imagination and scope of planners before Miliutin and to give some indication of the utopian thinking with which Soviet planners were preoccupied. At the same time, it is important to know what elements were on hand upon which Miliutin could draw in formulating his own theory.

Early Soviet theories of city planning are so closely intermeshed with those of pre-Revolutionary Russia that any clear distinction between the two stages is difficult to make. The two major cities which were determining influences in Russian ideas of city planning were Moscow and St. Petersburg, the Tsarist capital after the time of Peter the Great. Immediately following the 1917 Revolution, St. Petersburg, or, as it was renamed, Petrograd, was less influential in this respect than the new Bolshevik capital, Moscow, due to the classical influence in architectural style and city planning in the former capital, as well as its association with the Romanov dynasty.[7] Moscow's layout differed markedly from the Tsarist capital's classical plan, having grown concentrically about the ancient Russian citadel, the Kremlin. Radial arteries stretched from the Kremlin out toward the intercity highways. Suburbs and minor settlements had accumulated and expanded, as occasioned by population increases, and with the exception of a relatively few sections where conventional grid planning had been adopted, the development was sprawling and largely determined by land values and the location of factory buildings. This process held generally true until the adoption of the overall city plan of 1935. There were, however, earlier attempts on the part of pre-Revolutionary architects and engineers to deal with the mushrooming of residential buildings that industrialization and urbanization brought about in the city during the nineteenth century.

Early 1918 can be taken as the origin of Soviet town planning; at that time a decree of the Bolshevik Party socialized the land and opened the way to a multitude of proposals as to its proper use.[8] A special architectural workshop was formed by the Moscow City Soviet, under the direction of A. V. Shchusev and I. V. Zholtovskii, for the purposes of preserving ancient monuments and existing green areas and of preparing plans for slum clearance.[9] It was also proposed that an overall plan for the new capital be drawn up, but—due to the exigencies of civil war and famine—not much was accomplished beyond a few drawings, which still survive.[10]

Little advance was made in planning and housing during the first few years following the Revolution,[11] and early proposals for workers' settlements reflect a continuation of pre-Revolutionary practices. To cite only two examples, a workers' settlement for the Burnaev Chemical Plant, at Kishnema on the Volga River near Ivanovo,

had been built in 1915; and a cement factory, at Koktebel in the Crimea, which also provided for workers' housing, was partially complete at the time of the 1917 Revolution. Both complexes are examples of the work of the Vesnin brothers—Leonid (1880–1933), Viktor (1882–1940), and Aleksandr (1883–1959)—whose careers were to be of major significance later, during the 1920s.[12] The Vesnins were responsible as well for a post-Revolutionary plan for the Shatursk Power Station, which was among the first large-scale Soviet industrial projects, although in layout it was very similar to the earlier Burnaev and Koktebel works.[13] Such projects as Burnaev and Koktebel, although exceptional perhaps, were indicative of an enlightened approach in that they provided good dwellings for the factory workers, and of an efficient attitude, in that the siting of these dwellings made it possible for the workers to live near their work. In both cases, the plants were located near raw-material deposits.

This enlightened approach to housing was not, however, followed by most factory builders; the Russian reaction to industrialization reflects a lack of concern about the uglier aspects of it, and only in rare instances did the Russian builder realize that improving the lot of his workers could insure greater productivity. The urban housing crisis brought on by the Industrial Revolution in nineteenth-century Russia had been particularly severe owing to the dramatic movement of freed serfs away from the countryside. Speculation in land and extreme overcrowding due to the rapidly increasing urban worker population produced squalid slums and a restive, revolutionary

city proletariat.[14]

After 1917, various organizations attempted to deal with problems of planning and housing. By July of 1922, Western reformative ideas had taken root, to judge from a lecture given to one of these organizations by one Vladimir N. Semenov, on "Basic Principles of Garden Cities," and the slogan developed: "The Garden City—City of Liberated Labor."[15] In September 1922, the first garden city, sponsored by this same organization, was proposed for a site near Moscow to house 500 inhabitants. This was to have been financed partly through public subscription and partly through aid from the government in the form of lumber-rights concessions. Garden cities were also proposed for the cities of Tver' (1924), Ivanovo (1924), Briansk (1925), and elsewhere.[16]

An event of major significance in Russia shortly after the garden city proposals was the All-Union Agricultural and Handicrafts Industry Exhibition of 1923 (Pl. 3).[17] In the design of the various Exhibition pavilions playful use was made of avant-garde forms, and the fair was remarkable for the view it afforded visitors of the latest Soviet experimental architecture. In contrast to this progressive outlook in the matter of architectural style, the plan adopted for the disposition of the Exhibition buildings was a conservative one. The committee entrusted with planning the Exhibition chose a rather formal grid with cellular plots on the periphery to accommodate the various pavilions. The site later became Moscow's well-known Gor'kii Park, and the grid plan is still evident. The plan chosen by the committee was designed by the aforementioned Shchusev, who by this time was a leading member of MAO, the Moscow Society of Architects.

Among the exhibits at the 1923 fair was an area which illustrated the differences between traditional village life and that to be enjoyed in new Soviet settlements (Pl. 3, the lower portion, at the center of the plan).[18] This general type of small-scale workers' cooperative, composed of cottage-like dwellings, was characteristic of early Soviet plans for workers' settlements, and a number were built. Plates 4 and 5 illustrate one example: that of the Sokol (Falcon) suburb of Moscow, designed by N. V. Markovnikov and begun in 1923. A step away from this pleasant but impractical semirural type of cottage town is illustrated by L. A. Vesnin's design for a four-story apartment residence in 1924 (Pl. 6). Vesnin allotted the central part of the first floor to a communal dining room, kitchen, and library. This would have allowed for subsequent development in two different ways: either toward continued use for individual families living on a cooperative basis, or toward what was then thought of as "full" communism, that is to say, an aggregate of unmarried adults who would raise their children in common, without relying upon the family as the basic economic unit.

A slightly more conservative combination of the individual dwelling with a quasilinear plan is to be found in the Dukstroi settlement, built in 1924–25 for the Duks (Dux) Tobacco Plant in Moscow, and designed by V. I. Venderov. Its two-story houses, divided into four-, six-, and eight-apartment groups, were strung out along a tree-lined park on Begovaia Street (Pls. 7, 8).

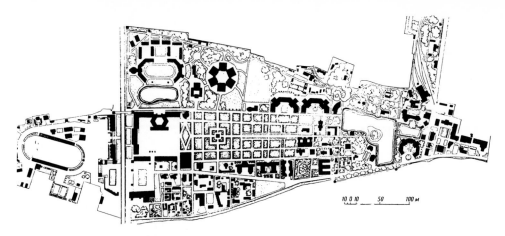

3. A. V. SHCHUSEV. PROJECT FOR THE ALL-RUSSIAN AGRICULTURAL AND HANDICRAFTS INDUSTRY EXHIBITION, MOSCOW, 1922–1925. REPRINTED FROM AFANAS'EV AND KHAZANOVA, *FROM THE HISTORY OF SOVIET ARCHITECTURE*, P. 175.

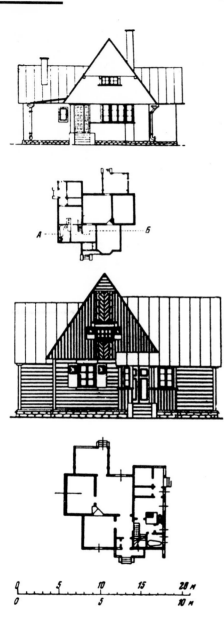

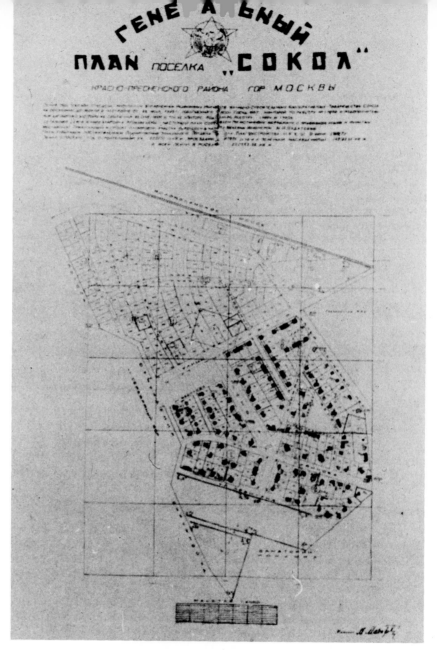

4. N. V. MARKOVNIKOV. SOKOL SUBURB PROJECT. 1923–1927. REPRINTED FROM AFANAS'EV AND KHAZANOVA, P. 56.

5. N. V. MARKOVNIKOV. SOKOL SUBURB PROJECT 1923–1927. INDIVIDUAL HOUSE. REPRINTED FROM AFANAS'EV AND KHAZANOVA, P. 57.

6. LEONID VESNIN. PROJECT FOR A COMMUNAL-TYPE HOUSE, 1924. REPRINTED FROM AFANAS'EV AND KHAZANOVA, P. 60.

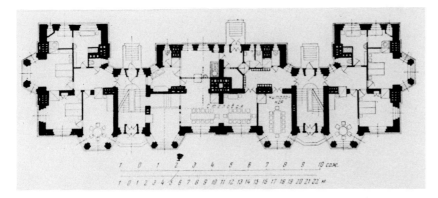

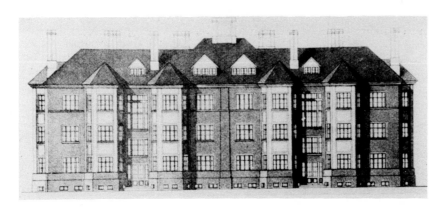

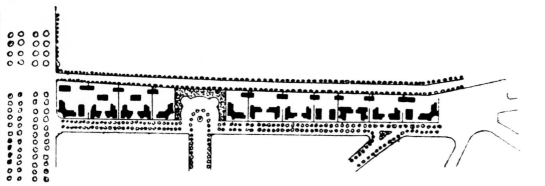

7. V. I. VENDEROV. PLAN FOR THE DUKSTROI SETTLEMENT, 1924–1925. REPRINTED FROM BYLINKIN ET AL., *HISTORY OF SOVIET ARCHITECTURE*, P. 54.

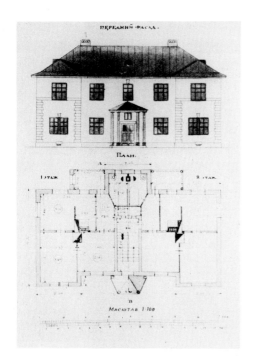

8. V. I. VENDEROV. DUKSTROI SETTLEMENT, 1924–1925. WORKERS' APARTMENT HOUSE. REPRINTED FROM AFANAS'EV AND KHAZANOVA, P. 59.

9. LEONID VESNIN. LENINSK SUBURB PROJECT (PART OF NEW MOSCOW), 1924. REPRINTED FROM AFANAS'EV AND KHAZANOVA, P. 45.

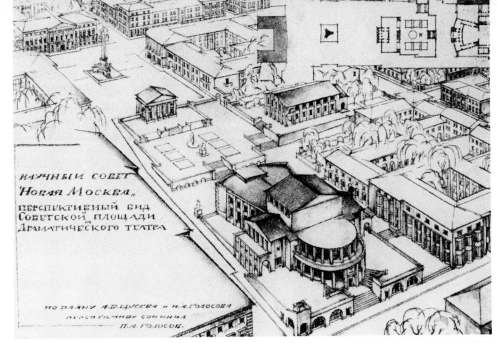

НАУЧНЫЙ СОВЕТ
"НОВАЯ МОСКВА"

ПЕРСПЕКТИВНЫЙ ВИД
СОВЕТСКОЙ ПЛОЩАДИ
ДРАМАТИЧЕСКОГО ТЕАТРА

ПО ПЛАНУ А.В.ЩУСЕВА и И.А.ГОЛОСОВА
ПЕРСПЕКТИВУ СОЧИНИЛ
И.А. ГОЛОСОВ.

10. I. A. GOLOSOV. NEW MOSCOW PROJECT, 1924. PERSPECTIVE OF SOVIET SQUARE AND THEATER.
REPRINTED FROM AFANAS'EV AND KHAZANOVA, P. 44.

An example of larger scale urban planning is Vesnin's project of January 1924 for the Leninsk suburb (Pl. 9), an informal and varied grouping of residential buildings, interspersed with ponds, parks, and monuments, which also seems to have incorporated an extensive trolley-track system through the main street and square. Vesnin's suburb project was to have been part of a larger overall plan for the capital, called New Moscow. This overall plan was undertaken in 1924 under the direction of Shchusev, following the success of his Exhibition plan of the previous year. A detail of the New Moscow project is seen in Pl. 10. This project seems to have consisted of a series of fanciful perspective renderings of various proposals for the replanning of the city centers and suburbs of Moscow; it was brought to completion by students of the Vkhutemas (the Higher Artistic-Technical Studios), with the cooperation and partial supervision of I. A. Golosov, a young and adventurous member of the Constructivist wing of Soviet architects.[19]

In the early 1920s a proposal had been put forth for the planning of Moscow by a Professor S. S. Shestakov, about whom little else is known. This was the so-called Greater Moscow Plan, and, while it received considerable publicity, it does not appear to have been government-sponsored, as Shchusev's New Moscow Plan had been (Pl. 11). Shestakov's plan provided for the growth of the capital into the world's greatest city, and allowed for the planting of huge areas of greenery, a ring development, and the preservation of ancient monuments.[20] The plan resembled a Greek cross inscribed within a circle with

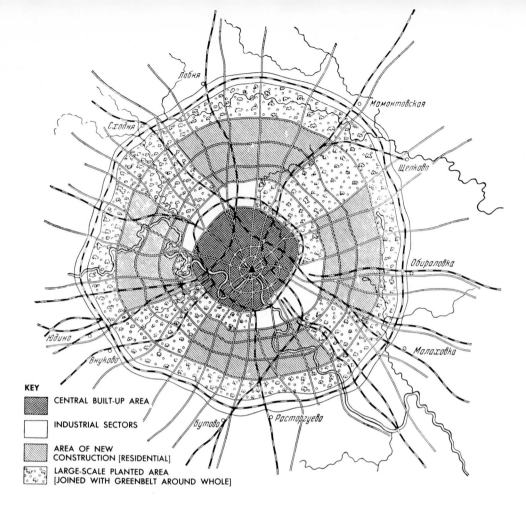

KEY

▨ CENTRAL BUILT-UP AREA

□ INDUSTRIAL SECTORS

▨ AREA OF NEW
CONSTRUCTION [RESIDENTIAL]

▨ LARGE-SCALE PLANTED AREA
[JOINED WITH GREENBELT AROUND WHOLE]

11. S. S. SHESTAKOV. GREATER MOSCOW PRO-
JECT, EARLY 1920S. REPRINTED FROM AFANAS'EV
AND KHAZANOVA, P. 49.

satellite cities outside the circumference. It
was published in the newspaper *Izvestiia* in
October 1925, and may possibly have
been influenced by Viennese theories of
planning. Three days after its publication,
the Office of the Moscow Guberniia (District) Engineer issued a new set of zoning
laws for the capital, which were published
in the same newspaper, and which closely
conformed to Shestakov's basic proposals.[21] The District Engineer, P. A. Mamatov,
divided the city into six belts:

- The Kremlin.
- Kitaigorod.
- From Kitaigorod to the Boulevard
  Ring and the Moscow River.
- From the Boulevard Ring to Sado-
  voe Kol'tso (the Garden Ring).
- From the Garden Ring to Kamer-
  Kollezhskogo.
- From Kamer-Kollezhskogo to the
  city limits.

Ancient monuments were to be preserved,
and all construction was limited to six-story
buildings, seventy-seven feet in height. Residences were limited to four stories, and
construction in the city center was permitted
only with government approval. This latter
practice was actually a direct echo of Tsarist building codes that had been in force in
the imperial capital since before 1840.[22]

Kaganovich, in his address to the
1931 Bolshevik Party Congress, commented
as follows about the Shestakov plan:

*In Moscow, particularly, we had not,
and still have not, a plan for the construction of new streets and the reconstruction of
old streets. There was the plan of the engineer Shestakov, known as the "Greater
Moscow Plan." But this was a mere paper*

plan drawn up without any regard for economic and social conditions. It was a product of the draughtsman's office. As an illustration of how little attention problems of scientific town planning receive, it should be noted that Communists working in the city enterprises, in spite of the fact that nobody had approved Shestakov's plans, nevertheless, when assigning sites for building purposes, guided themselves by this plan.[23]

Mamatov was further responsible for the publication of a Russian translation of Sitte's *City Planning according to Its Artistic Principles*, so that, while details are lacking, the ideas of Sitte would seem to have had some circulation in Moscow planning circles during the mid-1920s.[24] The Shestakov plan, Mamatov's zoning laws, and this publication of a text on city planning indicate a general impatience with official planning offices, whose work up to this point had produced little beyond a few cottage suburbs and Shchusev's attractive paper sketches of pretty city centers. Planners were obviously groping for ideas.

It was not until the beginning of the First Five-Year Plan in 1928 that the Soviet government took an active role in encouraging planners to work out new theories for the building of cities. Prior to 1928, under Lenin's New Economic Policy (NEP), which allowed a considerable degree of free enterprise in the USSR, architects and planners were primarily occupied with the design of individual buildings and problems of style.

Miliutin's Modernist Associations

The subject of the modern movement in Soviet architecture, and Constructivism in particular, has been treated in so many books, exhibitions, articles, and special issues of magazines in recent years that there is no need to survey it here, but only to mention certain aspects of the movement that were closely related to Miliutin and the formation of his book.[25]

Among the Russian architects, Miliutin seems to have been closest and in greatest sympathy with Moisei Ginzburg—who was in turn a friend and profound admirer of Le Corbusier, whom Miliutin had probably met in Moscow. As Finance Minister of the Russian Republic, Miliutin had commissioned in 1928 one of Ginzburg's most important buildings, the Domnarkomfin collective apartment house for workers in the Ministry, and we have mentioned that a number of Ginzburg's projects were illustrated in *Sotsgorod*. According to Le Corbusier, Miliutin lived in an apartment building designed by Ginzburg.[26]

Miliutin seems also to have favored the controversial and radical young architect Ivan Leonidov, illustrating his project for Magnitogorsk in *Sotsgorod*, albeit with some criticism, and later defending Leonidov in an article in his (Miliutin's) magazine as part of the continued polemic that raged over Leonidov's highly formalistic and considerably utopian designs (Pl. 12).

Miliutin was not happy with a number of Soviet architects. He leveled criticism at the old-line academicians, at the supporters of eclectic architecture (including his own superior, Anatolii Lunacharskii[27]), and at the extreme collectivists. In his later period

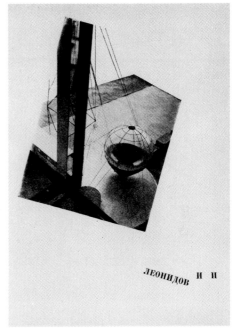

12. I. I. LEONIDOV. PROJECT FOR THE LENIN INSTITUTE, 1925, AS IT APPEARED IN *SOVREMENNAIA ARKHITECKTURA*, VOL. 1, NO. 4–5, 1926, P. 122.

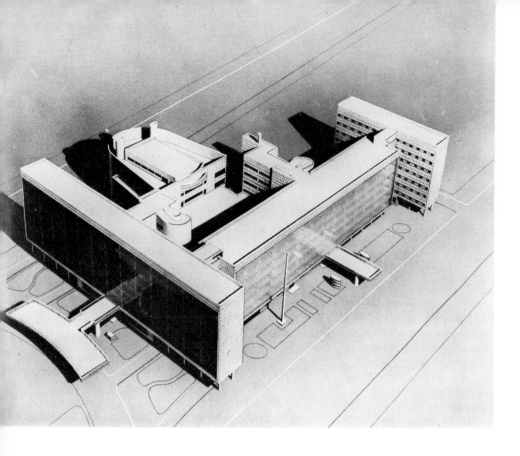

13. LE CORBUSIER. TSENTROSOIUZ, 1928–. RE-PRINTED FROM LE CORBUSIER, *OEUVRES COMPLETES*, VOL. I, 1910–1929, (ZURICH: GIRSBERGER; 4TH ED., 1946), P. 219.

14. LE CORBUSIER, TSENTROSOIUZ, 1928–. MAIN ENTRANCE. PHOTOGRAPH BY ARTHUR SPRAGUE.

of recantation he fired salvos at a number of others, like the disurbanist Okhitovich, largely for their political deviations.

Miliutin's ideas about architecture were so sympathetic with and influenced by the principles practiced by the Constructivist Ginzburg, that a few remarks about the latter might be in order.[28]

The son of an architect, Moisei Iak-ovlevich Ginzburg (1892–1946) traveled extensively and studied in Italy, as did many Russian architects; he was graduated in 1914 from the Academy in Milan and also earned a Russian engineering degree. He wrote constantly on the history and theory of architecture (some relevant publications of his are listed in our bibliography). By the early 1920s he was teaching at the Vkhutemas and at the Moscow Institute of Higher Technology and was a member of the Russian Academy of Arts and Sciences. In 1924 he published his major theoretical work, *Style and Epoch*, which includes a stylistic analysis of Constructivism that reflects his indebtedness to Le Corbusier on the one hand and cyclical theories of history on the other.[29] The book was, in fact, set up as a sort of socialist version of Le Corbusier's *Towards a New Architecture*, and it indicates that Ginzburg was already under the spell of the Swiss architect—an enthusiasm that he was soon to pass on to his fellow Russians and which culminated in the invitation to Le Corbusier to design the Tsentrosoiuz (administrative center for Soviet trade unions—later changed to the Commissariat of Light Industry) in Moscow in 1928–29 (Pls. 13, 14; Fig. 92). Constructivism, of course, was not simply an avant-garde outgrowth of the International Style, but had evolved out of the theories of Malevich, Tatlin, Lissitzky, and others and was fraught with social propaganda of a decidedly Soviet cast.

In 1928, when the choice of architect for an apartment house for the workers of the Finance Ministry was to be made, Ginzburg was assigned the commission. The result was Domnarkomfin, or, as it is popularly known, the "Ship House." [30] Domnarkomfin was planned on socialist principles of collectivization, but was designed in the spirit of Le Corbusier's work (Pls. 15–19). It is a multi-story dwelling that, as originally planned, went much further with collectivized services than our previous example, that of Vesnin (Pl. 6). [31] That Domnarkomfin was built as a nearly completely collectivized dwelling heralds the changeover in 1928 from Lenin's NEP to the institution of the First Five-Year Plan and socialist "reconstruction," which presumed a full-scale conversion to State-planned economy and the collectivization of agriculture. Whether the specific innovations in the programming of the Domnarkomfin represented ideas of Miliutin or of Ginzburg is not known, but the close collaboration that the construction of Domnarkomfin must have entailed surely exposed Miliutin to this most progressive Soviet architect and would account for much that Miliutin discussed later in *Sotsgorod.*

In 1925 Ginzburg and the brothers Vesnin had formed OSA (the Union of Contemporary Architects), a group of Constructivists who were presumably more concerned with practical matters like housing, engineering structure, and industrialized building methods than the existing avant-

15. M. IA. GINZBURG. DOMNARKOMFIN, (APARTMENT HOUSE FOR THE MINISTRY OF FINANCE, CHAIKOVSKII STREET, MOSCOW), 1928. REPRINTED FROM *ARCHITECTURAL REVIEW*, VOL. 71, MAY 1932, P. 204.

16. M. IA. GINZBURG. DOMNARKOMFIN, 1928. EXTERIOR. PHOTOGRAPH BY ARTHUR SPRAGUE.

19. M. IA. GINZBURG. DOMNARKOMFIN, 1928. CONNECTED BUILDING FOR COLLECTIVIZED SERVICES—CAFETERIA, LAUNDRY, ETC. PHOTOGRAPH BY ARTHUR SPRAGUE.

17. M. IA. GINZBURG. DOMNARKOMFIN, 1928. CLOSE-UP OF CONNECTING PASSAGEWAY. PHOTOGRAPH BY ARTHUR SPRAGUE.

18. M. IA. GINZBURG. DOMNARKOMFIN, 1928. INTERIOR CORRIDOR. PHOTOGRAPH BY ARTHUR SPRAGUE.

garde group ASNOVA, which was of a somewhat more formalist extraction. From 1926 to 1930, under the editorship of Ginzburg and the Vesnins, the group published *SA* (*Sovremennaia Arkhitektura: Contemporary Architecture*)—one of the most internationally admired periodicals of its day—whose pages have provided many of the illustrations for recent exhibitions of the Soviet movement. Perhaps the most official action of the OSA group came through its participation in Stroikom (Construction Committee of the RSFSR) a building research unit which it had pressed the government to set up under Ginzburg's direction in 1928 in order to study methods of standardization in housing. Projects by both OSA and Stroikom are cited and illustrated throughout *Sotsgorod*, and Miliutin drew continually on illustrations from *SA;* al-

though he seems to have admired their efforts in general, he was quite critical of oversights in their planning, where he saw them.

OSA during 1930–31 became SASS (Architects' Association for Socialist Construction), but it did not survive the general suppression of independent artistic societies in 1932. *SA* (*Contemporary Architecture*) ceased publication with its fifth anniversary number in 1930 and was followed from 1931–34 by another *SA* (*Sovetskaia Arkhitektura: Soviet Architecture*) of which Miliutin was editor. The dramatic Suprematist-Constructivist graphic design that had characterized its predecessor was toned down in the later magazine, and a change in intellectual climate became noticeable, as we shall see.

Miliutin's Life

Who was Nikolai Aleksandrovich Miliutin and what was his background in planning and politics? (Pl. 20)

In 1929 Nikolai Aleksandrovich Miliutin left a post as Minister of Finance of the RSFSR in order to devote himself to the study of town planning. His background in the Communist Party had been largely in bureaucratic posts in the social services of the new State.[32] A native of St. Petersburg (born 1889), where he grew up, he had early become a Party member and had operated as a Bolshevik agitator in industrial plants and in the army during the First World War.

Following the Revolution he served in a number of organizations that explain his later interest in supporting-services for the population and in statistical analysis of current problems. Several of these occupations can be seen to correspond to his publications of 1918–21. In March 1917 he was a member of the Petrograd Workers' Insurance Center; in December of that year he became Chairman of the Citywide Petrograd Hospital Accounting Office. He was also a member of Guprosovet (Provincial Food Supply Committee), a member of Ispolcomsovet (Executive Communist Soviet), and representative of the Commissariat of Labor Communes for the Northern Provinces. In 1918 he became a member of the College of the People's Commissariat of Labor. During 1920–21 he was Extraordinary Agent for the All-Union Central Executive Committee and Labor and Defense Council for Orlov and Voronezh, as well as Vice-Chairman of the People's Committee for Food Supply in the Ukraine during a ter-

20. PHOTOGRAPH OF N. A. MILIUTIN PRINTED IN HIS MAGAZINE *SOVETSKAIA ARKHITEKTURA* IN 1932. REPRINTED FROM VOL. 2, 1932, NO. 5–6, P. 17.

rible famine there. From 1922–24 he was acting People's Commissar for the Commissariat of Social Security of the RSFSR, and then was promoted to the position of People's Commissar (i.e., Minister) of Finance for the RSFSR. Thus he came to his planning studies with a fairly comprehensive grasp of administrative and service problems of the USSR.

Miliutin's growing reputation, through his Party background, for his ability to deal with problems of living conditions under the new way of life, and his position as a leader among the architectural *cognoscenti* was apparently what led, in 1929, to the offer of the chairmanship of a study committee on the construction of new cities, which was being formed by the Communist Academy. Originally the Socialist Academy, this organization has been described as follows:

Although a completely official body, subordinated to the Central Executive Committee, the Communist Academy nevertheless retained until 1927–28, a large measure of aloofness from the strife going on in the party. . . . The intellectual activity of the Academy during this period was the golden age of Marxist thought in the USSR. A number of stimulating works appeared under the auspices of the Academy in which the leading Marxists of the party, writing from different points of view, attempted to develop the principles of Marxism in the conditions applicable to Russia. Very few of these intellectuals were destined to survive the more rigorous control which would be applied to the Academy after NEP had been abandoned.[33]

As regards his qualifications to dis-

course on art and architecture, which he did, Miliutin was not really an architect, but had attended an art school part-time between 1905 and 1912. It was not until 1940 that he took a State examination and received an architectural degree.

Early in 1930 he contributed a brief essay to B. Lunin's remarkable little anthology of opinions about socialist cities and about the socialist reconstruction of the mode of living—a writing that indicates the direction in which his Academy study was going and which anticipates certain aspects of the forthcoming book *Sotsgorod*. The essay, which reads like a lecture, was entitled "The struggle for a new mode of life and Soviet urbanism." Among the fifteen other theorists who contributed (some of them more than one essay) were Lenin's widow N. K. Krupskaia, G. E. Zinoviev (one of Lenin's controversial heirs), Lunacharskii, L. Sabsovich (the radical urbanist), M. Okhitovich (the radical disurbanist), and other prominent architects, including Ginzburg, V. Zelenko, and A. Pasternak. The essays dealt with a variety of problems and opinions concerning the future of the city in the USSR and with current practices in collectivization, planning, and construction. Miliutin treated the latter. He insisted that the increased magnitude of projects in the Five-Year Plan called for an abandonment of outdated bourgeois ideas and values. Collectivized services, new construction techniques (as used by modern architects in the West), new norms (such as those of Stroikom and of the Domnarkomfin apartments), and a rationalization of the labor force—particularly as regards the place of women —are all obligatory. Old-line architects must cease labeling the young progressive architects as Trotskyites and counter-revolutionaries. As he said, "We have to build our new world."

With the publication of *Sotsgorod*, Miliutin obviously became a force to be reckoned with in the Party apparatus, and he was assigned as editor of *Sovetskaia Arkhitektura* which was published by the Commissariat of Public Education (Narkompros), of which he was a deputy commissar by virtue of his research project for the Communist Academy. He wrote occasional short articles on technical subjects for the magazine and a number of important pieces which are discussed in some detail below. He also published a couple of his own projects. The magazine terminated with the first issue of 1934, an issue whose frontispiece dealt not with architecture but with more ominous matters (Pl. 21). It had already been more or less superseded by *Arkhitektura SSSR* (*Architecture USSR*) and *Akademiia Arkhitektury*.

The following year Miliutin was made head of Kinofikatsiia (The Central Board of Film Distribution), a position that appears to have been something of an administrative sinecure. We are told that he continued to work on the subject of new towns, and there is some evidence that he kept in touch with his contacts abroad; but we know of no further important activities on his part, except that in 1939 he was serving as chief of the artistic section for the construction of the Palace of the Soviets in Moscow.[34] He died in 1942 at the age of 53. For the critical period 1930–34, The Soviet Encyclopedia merely lists him as "representative of the People's Commissariat of Public Education RSFSR."

Советская архитектура

L'ARCHITECTURE SOVIÉTIQUE
SOVIET ARCHITEKTURE
SOWJETISCHE ARCHITEKTUR

1 [19]
1934

21. TITLE-PAGE HEADING AND FACING FRONTISPIECE OF THE LAST ISSUE OF MILIUTIN'S MAGAZINE. *SOVETSKAIA ARKHITEKTURA*, VOL. 4, 1934, NO. 1.

Miliutin's Major Precepts and Possible Sources for His Ideas

In reading *Sotsgorod* we can sense several things about the author's ideals and the temper of the times. He spoke from more than a decade's experience in the planning and budgeting of public services, as we know. He had statistics at his fingertips and was up to date on the latest census-type studies and policy directives of various official commissions. He had done extensive research on the new architecture since his appointment to the governmental commission on town planning, and he was attuned to the latest theory and practice in Russia and elsewhere. All this perhaps makes Miliutin out to be a bit mechanical and technocratic and we have been perhaps a bit condescending to call him a "functionary," when actually all evidence points to a warm sincerity on his part and a total dedication to the ideal of gradual socialist transformation of the Russian life style. Certainly he showed a deep affection and consideration for children, their care, and their education.

Amongst the intellectuals in the USSR there still persisted in the late 1920s a state of euphoria about the future of the working class for whom the architects, planners, and other technicians were designing housing and communal facilities. It was assumed that these proletarian workers, given a minimally comfortable environment, would develop valuable modern skills on the job and in technical schools and would grow in community consciousness in the clubs and various collective facilities provided for their leisure time. As Anatole Kopp writes, "Like electrical condensers that transform the na-ture of current, the architects' proposed 'social condensers' were to turn the self-centered individual of capitalist society into a whole man, the informed militant of socialist society in which the interests of each merged with the interests of all."[35] But Party intellectuals like Miliutin were writing prescriptions for a future order of classless socialism that the mass of workers would never realize. Far from developing as effective agents in their own right, the workers were to become essentially cogs in a State managed by a new class—the Party bureaucracy—which in turn was to be shaped to form under Stalinist purges. But our purpose here is not to bemoan the eventual estrangement of the Party and the working class in the USSR, but rather to communicate the deep sense of mission and the high idealism that marked the agitated years in which Miliutin's book was composed.[36]

The 14 chapters of his book are organized in a rational argumentation, proceeding from the most general problems to the specifics of his plan on the one hand and the economics of construction and budget on the other. We will discuss the sections sequentially below, but, cutting across them for the moment, it is useful to analyze his message in terms of (1) those of his ideas that were typical of the moment, (2) the position that he occupied on controversial matters, (3) his unique contributions, and (4) some of his sources.

He called for new constructional forms for the new circumstances—not merely for renovation and efficiency as did Le Corbusier—because the old forms and systems were a function of bourgeois capitalistic society and had been determined by the dy-namics of the marketplace. He strove for the abolition of the distinction between urban and rural life, repeatedly quoting Marxist authority on the matter. He wrote in great detail about the "living cell" and illustrated it with his own models (Figs. 21–23, 65–72). The living cell was a basic residential unit for all housing, of a type that the CIAM was then studying and calling *"Existenzminimum."* [37] The complement to the living cell is a wealth of supporting services, all collectivized for economy and efficiency: clubs, libraries, canteens, recreational rooms, laundries, nurseries, repair shops, and the like. The collectivization of certain of these services would bring about the emancipation of woman, especially from housework, a matter on which Miliutin dwells often and quotes extensively about from the *Communist Manifesto.* This liberation of woman through collectivized services would allow her to become a member of the productive labor force, along with other dependents. Finally, Miliutin goes into exacting detail about the facilities for education of children and youths. It is in this that his book resembles most strongly—and that he drew consciously or unconsciously upon—the utopian socialist programs of the nineteenth century. All the precepts enumerated here were fairly standard among Soviet theorists of the day.[38]

In his advocacy of these measures we have mentioned that Miliutin assumed a "realistic" middle way; his second chapter is entitled "The Avoidance of Extremes." [39] He points out that "We have now neither the technology nor the material means" that will be achieved in the future fully-developed socialism (Chap. 2). And although

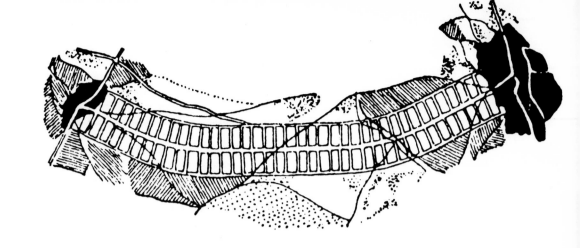

22. THE SPANISH LINEAR CITY AS ILLUSTRATED IN EL LISSITZKY'S *RUSSLAND* OF 1930. REPRINTED FROM EL LISSITZKY, *RUSSIA: AN ARCHITECTURE FOR WORLD REVOLUTION.*

he condemns capitalist cities, he comments, "Does it follow . . . that the now-existing cities, settlements, etc., as well as routes of communication must be altogether ignored? Of course not. . . . We cannot throw into the trash basket indiscriminately everything that we have inherited from the past. We must transform and assimilate this heritage . . ." (Chap. 4). On the matter of the institution of the family he is somewhat ambiguous. Following Marx and Engels, he considers the family to be evil as an economic institution: "People's intimate relationships will become their own private affairs independent of any direct property considerations" (Chap. 8). With "The New Organization of Life" (as he calls his Chap. 6) the "family mode of life" will be phased out. Nevertheless, he considers parent-child relationships to be important and insists that collective feeding and education will not take children away from their parents (Chap. 6). In all these matters Miliutin was in line with the just-published Bolshevik Party resolution (see his App. 2) which condemned certain visionary plans not so much

for their deviation in physical structure and form as for their being totally out of line with the current economic and social conditions in Russia (i.e., in the working class). Miliutin's remarks about agriculture are curiously limited, considering the role that it plays in his ideal layout; very little rural planning seems to have been done in this period of Soviet development.[40]

His really unique contribution is, of course, the linear industrial settlement plan (Figs. 11, 14, 16). There were antecedents, which fact Miliutin was probably aware of, but as it is decidedly different from them and as he suggests no prototype for it, it is fair to assume that he really invented it. The idea of linear planning itself was apparently popular with the Russian disurbanists, and the plan of the Spanish linear city was known to them.[41] The Spanish linear city (Pl. 22) did not involve the principle of segregated functions; Garnier's plan (Pl. 2) did just that, but was not linear and the functions were segregated in clumps—not in any relation to the boulevard that served as axis to his residential sector. Miliutin's

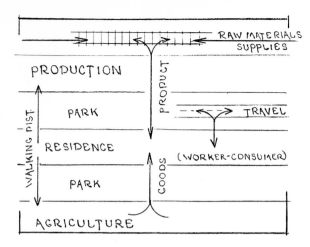

RAW MATERIALS SUPPLIES

PRODUCTION

PARK

TRAVEL

RESIDENCE

(WORKER-CONSUMER)

PARK

AGRICULTURE

23. N. A. MILIUTIN'S CITY, PROVIDING PROXIMITY OF RESIDENCE TO BOTH PRODUCTION AND AGRICULTURE. DIAGRAM BY ARTHUR SPRAGUE.

schema combines major features of these two plans but in a way that seems rather to grow out of his reasoning process about industrial efficiency and residential communities.

As an industrial settlement is for the purpose of productive output, its most logical arrangement, Miliutin argues, is a continuous one with one process leading to the next as in a steam power plant;[42] subsidiary processes and input mechanisms should be arranged parallel and flanking the main processes as in an assembly line. Intersecting processes are to be avoided at all costs.[43] Residences for workers should be insulated from noise and smoke of the factories by a green zone to be set up in a band parallel to the factories so that work is at an easy walking distance for all. The green belt would contain the main highway, thus insulating the residences from it and from the railway that passes back of the factories. The landscaped residential zone would have in it all the schools and nonmanufacturing social services, which would in turn be available to nearby farms and villages—in line with the Marxist tenet of bringing the urban and rural together (Pl. 23).

Once stated, Miliutin's schema is so obvious that it is no wonder that it turns up in nearly every book on modern city planning. But only by reading his text would one realize how carefully he has rationalized and calculated all the secondary processes that go on in each zone. Capacities of canteens, schools, nurseries, etc., are worked out by careful statistical study of the composition of the work force and the average size of families. Siting and interconnections

of the buildings are based on a study of servant-served relationships of the units. There are also certain principles that do not show up in the diagrams. He insists on the use of standardized building elements composed of economic materials of a life span that will not, in factories, outlast the machines that they are to house. He also calculates the relative economy of collective over individual services (as in laundries) and stresses the savings that accrue by designing in modern unmonumental terms. Miliutin underscores the economy inherent in the low buildings that his plan will allow instead of multifloor factories or skyscrapers which he calls "the peak—the last cry of capitalism."[44]

Although Miliutin would have us believe that his ideas were formulated only in terms of the "analysis of K. Marx, F. Engels, and V. I. Lenin," an appreciable amount of his thinking came directly from American sources. He was extremely interested in American industrial methodology, in particular, the assembly-line system. That Miliutin was adapting American methods to the layout of his system is clear in his choice of terms: he described his linear town as a "functional assembly line."[45]

Not only in recent times, but from the very first years of the Revolution, the Soviets have measured themselves against the United States in matters of production. Long before diplomatic relations were established officially (the United States recognized the USSR only in 1933), Soviet missions were sent to the United States to acquire the technical information and assistance necessary to industrialize their new society. In this, the Ford Company represented the pinnacle of success; "fordizatsiia" (Fordization) was in vogue, especially during the 1920s, as a term for accomplished planning in every field from industrial programs to students' study habits. As New Russia's Primer described the assembly-line system (p. 75): "Men stand still, but things move." One of the earliest major plants in the USSR that used the assembly line was the Stalingrad Tractor Plant, which manufactured Fordson tractors.[46] Prior to the construction of the city of Magnitogorsk, this plant was given wide publicity as evidence of socialist progress. The factory at Stalingrad was actually prefabricated in Detroit by the Albert Kahn Company and shipped to the USSR in 1929, where it was assembled under the direction of American engineers.[47] Both Stalingrad and Magnitogorsk are discussed by Miliutin in his fifth chapter.

The part played by American companies in the early phases of industrialization in the USSR is a little publicized chapter in the history of US–Soviet relations. Americans were hired to travel about the USSR, supervising major construction and training construction workers on the spot. One company opened a drafting office in Moscow, and American help was directly involved in the building of over fifty major enterprises in some thirty Soviet cities by the Kahn Company alone.[48] One plant, the Avtostroi automobile factory (Molotov Works) at Nizhninovgorod (now Gor'kii), also discussed in Miliutin's Chap. 5, was designed under supervision of the Ford Company itself.[49] Both Ginzburg and Miliutin—as well as any interested Soviet planner or architect who read German—had direct access to Henry

Ford's ideas through the 1923 Leipzig translation of his biography, *My Life and Work*.[50] However, it should be pointed out that no mention of Ford's name appears in *Sotsgorod*.

Another unnamed prototype for Miliutin's process-thinking was the Taylor System of shop management. Frederick Winslow Taylor (1856–1915), a pioneer in industrial efficiency and scientific management in the United States, was one of the first to try to cut production costs by a more efficient use of productive equipment. His principles of scientific management, based on time studies and standardization of processes, spread throughout the industrialized countries; a Taylor Society was founded in 1915. "Taylor was the first really to grasp that work could become an object of science. He pursued this concept with great energy and brilliance into a vision of a new technocratic Jerusalem; and the ideas he advanced were necessary for the transition between the old preindustrial system and today's world of automation. Even Lenin exhorted the new Soviet society to make use of Taylorism. His achievement thus parallels Ford's mastery of mass production in historical significance."[51]

The immediate or specific *Soviet* guidelines that Miliutin followed were: the pronouncements of Joseph Stalin, from which he quotes repeatedly; a Gosplan study of manpower and social services at Magnitogorsk (included as his App. 1); and the 1930 Bolshevik Party Congress Resolution "Concerning the work of reconstructing our way of life" (his App. 2), which we have cited above.

As for architectural style (the subject of his Chap. 12), he drew strictly on the Le Corbusier and Bauhaus traditions except for a curious Scheerbartian comment about the new city serving as a beacon for airplanes (see p. 71 of the present volume).

●

The Content of *Sotsgorod*

At this point it may be useful to analyze the construction and the content of Miliutin's book.

The Foreword was contributed by N. Meshcheriakov, chairman of the board of the *Larger Soviet Encyclopedia* (*Bol'shaia Sovetskaia Entsiklopediia*) and for nearly two decades chief editor of the *Shorter Soviet Encyclopedia* (*Malaia Sovetskaia Entsiklopediia*). He warns that the construction to be carried out in the Soviet Union in the course of its industrialization cannot follow either traditional methods or capitalist speculative procedures. He regrets that the current excitement about city planning in the USSR does not have a substantial body of literature to depend upon. He recommends Miliutin's book as just such a knowledgeable source and commends it for stressing new rather than obsolete techniques and yet avoiding visionary and presently impossible solutions.

This is precisely the character of the book, as we have noted, and is what the author himself, in his preface, promises to do; Miliutin strongly urges the establishment of an experimental institute of urban design to focus on problems such as are raised in the book. He claims to have made an intense study of current theory and practice in Russia and the West and to have familiarized himself with the reports of pertinent Soviet agencies. In line with what we will see to be a new tendency—to correlate architecture and planning theory with Marxist polity—he stresses that he has limited himself to those aspects of his subject that derive from the ideas of Marx, Engels, and Lenin, that is, he concerns himself with the socialist city, as implied by his title.[52]

His first chapter, "The Essence of the Problem," sets out in general terms what is to be accomplished in the USSR with regard to new settlements and old cities during the First Five-Year Plan. Available funds must be employed with great efficiency through the use of new construction technology and must be directed toward the socialist transformation of the way of life, most specifically in the freeing of women from "domestic slavery." In particular, the pitfalls of capitalist speculative procedures must be avoided—especially urban concentration and skyscraper development.

"The Avoidance of Extremes" (Chap. 2) underscores the dangers of disregarding present circumstances and planning mindlessly as if fully developed socialism were already in existence. He urges an increase in labor productivity and a consequent raising of the living standard, the housing accommodation, and the cultural level of workers and peasants. His theme of a middle way, or rather a dialectic resolution of rival theories is developed in Chap. 3, "Urbanization or Disurbanization?" He describes the Western dilemma of first having centralized industry and trade at points (cities), which has engendered the dreadful workers' slums of the capitalist world, and of now trying either to disperse in garden cities (which he considers to be impossible under the system of capitalism) or to tinker with technological services in the cities (from which improvements the proletariat derives little benefit). He finds current Soviet controversies over centralization or decentralization to be irrelevant because "the modern city is a product of mercantile society and will die together with it, merging into the socialist industrialized countryside" as the differences between city and country are eliminated. Marx, Engels, and Lenin prophesied just that, and he cites them at length.

In Chap. 4, "Choosing Sites for New Construction," Miliutin again castigates capitalist cities. He calls for a halt to the continued industrialization of presently existing cities and recommends planning in terms of a more rational relation to sources of materials, agricultural production, and new power grids (citing Lenin on this). On the other hand he emphasizes, as we have seen, that existing cities, settlements, and communication routes are not to be ignored; any expansion of them, however, should be done with forethought. The "industrialization of agriculture," he warns, does not mean scattering small-scale industry about; both industry and agriculture must take advantage of large-scale mechanized production.

Chapter 5, "Principles of Planning," is a description of Miliutin's model, and it develops logically out of all the foregoing. He leads off with the analogy of the industrial part of a city to a large-scale steam-operated power plant, and describes, by comparison, the chaotic arrangements in improperly planned establishments. He then enumerates 10 basic factors to be considered in the layout of an industrial town: (1) interrelated production facilities and transportation arteries arranged according to a "flowing functional-assembly-line system"; (2) an adjacent residential zone for the workers, insulated by a greenbelt buffer; (3) railway lines adjoining the factories and a highway in the greenbelt to service both industry and residences; (4) a nearby agricultural area; (5) institutions for higher technical and agricultural education located close to the activities that they serve; (6) medical establishments; (7) primary schools; (8) service industries in the industrial zone; (9) warehouses; and (10) a planned program for demolition of inadequate residential units.

He then outlines a six-part linear pattern for the layout of these functions (Pl. 23), which arises quite inevitably from the way in which he categorized the functions themselves. He insists that any alteration in the sequence of the bands would inhibit both the growth and the operation of the various parts. Bodies of water and prevailing winds should be taken into account, but topographical features are generally irrelevant. He proceeds then, at some length and with a variety of diagrams, to use his linear plan with its functional-assembly-line organization of the factory elements as the basis for a critique of three famous Soviet industrial installations then under construction or recently completed.

For the new steel center of Magnitogorsk, for which a competition had been held, he discusses the prize project (Fig. 8), a plan (Fig. 9) submitted by OSA (actually designed by Leonidov), a plan (Fig. 10) submitted by Stroikom (the semiofficial organization headed by Ginzburg), and his own "assembly-line" model (Fig. 11). His criticisms of the first three are clearly enumerated in his text and need not be repeated here.

The entirely new city of Magnitogorsk was to become one of the greatest steel producing centers in the world. The name is derived from "magnitnaiia gora" ("magnetic mountain"), a mountain of such high-grade ore that in ancient times travelers noted a deflection of compass needles in the vicinity; hence the name "magnetic." Prior to the Revolution the ore had been only superficially mined and refined at the nearby Beloretskii plant; but now, under the First Five-Year Plan, the Soviets intended to develop the area into an extensive steel center and to lay out a new city to house the thousands of workers of the labor force.

Miliutin's proposal (Fig. 11) was organized as a section of his linear town and conforms to his six-zone division. He left out provisions for agriculture here, but we may assume that this band was to have occupied the opposite bank of the river, away from the town (lower part of Fig. 11). He would also have dammed the river to provide for a recreational water basin.

Of the other proposals for Magnitogorsk discussed by Miliutin, the most interesting is that put forward by the OSA. This would appear to be a schematic version (for the purpose of comparison) of a project drawn up by a younger member of that organization, Leonidov, whom we have referred to earlier. Miliutin also reproduced Leonidov's plan for Magnitogorsk elsewhere in *Sotsgorod* (Figs. 56–61), but without attributing it directly to him; although several detailed drawings accompany it, it is simply presented as the "settlement proposed by the OSA." This may, in part, have been a deliberate maneuver on Miliutin's part, in order that the controversial architect's name not be given such a prominent place in the book. Leonidov's Magnitogorsk plan appears to be long and quite narrow, incorporating rectangular park areas and a fanciful, pyramidal palace of culture. Our Pl. 24 shows a highly imaginative juxtaposition, probably Leonidov's own, of an actual photograph of a dirigible placed to show the airship flying over Magnitogorsk as drawn in the Leonidov plan—a typical Soviet use of photomontage.

None of the competition projects were taken seriously by the committee set up for the construction of Magnitogorsk, and, in 1930, the German planner, Ernst May, was invited to submit a possible solution. May's plan consisted of more conventional superblock neighborhood units with their buildings arranged in rows, the units stamped on the countryside with little regard for continuity in movement or for topography (Pl. 25). However, this was drastically altered after his departure from Russia.[53]

It was for the purpose of criticizing the existing tractor-assembly settlement at Stalingrad (which we have discussed above) that Miliutin devised his famous plan (Fig. 14). The other plans he illustrates in his discussion of Stalingrad were the actual situation as it had been laid out (Fig. 12), and a plan, otherwise unknown, prepared by a Stalingrad construction committee for the project (Fig. 13). Stalingrad was readily adaptable to a linear plan, due to its being strung out along the bank of the Volga. Miliutin's plan places the residential zone next to the river and follows his standard six-zone layout. His description of the plan is minimal, and he devotes most of this section to criticism of the plans of the others which followed the more conventional linear arrangement—like an American mill

за советское
мощное
дирижаблестроение

24. I. I. LEONIDOV. MAGNITOGORSK. PHOTO-
MONTAGE, CAPTIONED "ZA SOVETSKOE MOSHCH-
NOE DIRIZHABLESTROENIE" ("FOR MIGHTY
SOVIET DIRIGIBLE CONSTRUCTION"). FROM *SOV-
REMENNAIA ARKHITEKTURA*, VOL. 5, 1930, NO. 4,
P. 1.

town—of placing the factories at the waterside, presumably to use the river for transportation, for which Russian waterways serve to a very large extent.[54] As we can see from our Pl. 26, Traktorstroi (No. 2 in the plan) was only one of several industrial settlements that made up the Stalingrad riverfront prior to its destruction in the battle of World War II.

Miliutin's third, and most elaborately detailed model plan (Fig. 16) was intended for Avtostroi, the automobile plant at Nizhninovgorod which was designed in Detroit by Soviet engineers under the direction of the Ford Motor Co. and was being built in 1930–31 by the Austin Engineering Co. of Cleveland, Ohio (Fig. 15). Miliutin gives a particularly sweeping damnation of the factory layout. He goes to the greatest length in his criticism of Ford's plan, presumably because he is disillusioned to find the master of the assembly line not using his own principles for town planning. It is unlikely that Miliutin knew that Ford himself was a devotee of the linear plan and had proposed linear settlements for the Muscle Shoals area in the early 1920s. So far as is known, however, Ford was concerned primarily with electrification, with home craft and farming for the factory workers, and with the sale of his car–truck–Fordson tractor package to the residents; Ford apparently never developed the analogy between linear planning and his assembly line.

The author concludes this key chapter with a rehearsal of the advantages of the linear-conveyor system, of low rather than high-rise industrial plants, and of industrial buildings of short life span.

Chapter 6, "The New Organization of Life," is intended to reveal the ultimate purpose of Miliutin's plan as a social mechanism, and hence it deals with the residential aspects of his model. It is a rambling chapter in which he shadow-boxes with the current controversial question of the elimination of the family as an institution, and he quotes at great length from Marxist authority on that subject. He provides a special three-paragraph conclusion at the end of the chapter, however, which somewhat clarifies his points. The basic question is whether the present transitional stage of socialism is better served by collectivized services or by an improvement in existing individual facilities. He considers that the answer lies in the imminent need to increase the labor force, which can be done most economically by freeing woman from "domestic slavery" through the use of collectivized feeding arrangements and provisions for child care. This would in turn reduce the flow of workers to the city and reduce the demand for housing units. It would increase the income of families and hence their standard of living and culture. In time the orientation of life around the individual family would be replaced by a more social, collective ambient for the upbringing of children. Specifically, in residential areas the author calls for collective dining rooms with related reading and recreational rooms; nurseries, kindergartens, and dormitories for older children; laundries and repair shops; clubs and cultural facilities.

The remaining chapters of the book are concerned with elaborating details of the author's basic premise—collectivization—and of his model—the sectored linear plan. Chapter 7, "The Location of

Buildings," very brief, is really concerned with their orientation for proper sunlight, their disposition in efficient lines, and the avoidance of multiple use in residential buildings. Chapter 8, "The Living Cell," describes in detail the basic dwelling unit that we have discussed above, illustrating his thesis with projects of his own and of Stroikom (i.e., Ginzburg). He discusses the necessary dimensions, lists the minimal conveniences that should be provided, and ridicules those who would reduce the living cell to a "sleeping cabin," i.e., a bunk and little else.

The next two chapters deal with the buildings for the "Collectivized Institutions for the Needs of the Population," as the title of Chap. 9 reads. Most of Chap. 9 is spent in careful calculation of the capacities of nurseries, kindergartens, and various dormitories for the young. He concludes

25. ERNST MAY. PLAN FOR MAGNITOGORSK, 1933. FROM MINERVIN, G. B., ED., *MAGNITOGORSK*, FIG. 4, P. 20.

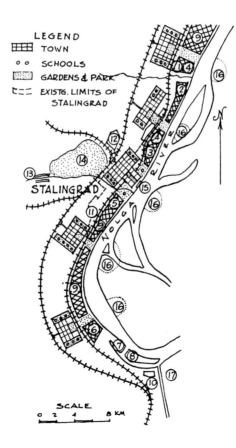

LEGEND
▦ TOWN
○ ○ SCHOOLS
▨ GARDENS & PARK
⊏⊐ EXISTG. LIMITS OF STALINGRAD

SCALE
0 2 1 8 KM

26. EARLY LINEAR PLAN FOR THE WHOLE OF STALINGRAD, 1929. FIVE COMMUNITIES GROUPED AROUND FIVE INDUSTRIAL COMBINES AND SURROUNDED BY AGRICULTURAL ZONES AND TRUCK FARMS. 1, AUTOMOTIVE PLANTS; 2, TRACTOR PLANTS; 3, METALWORKING PLANTS; 4, METALLURGICAL PLANTS; 5, FOOD INDUSTRY; 6, CHEMICAL PLANTS AND ELECTRIC STATIONS; 7, LUMBER MILLS; 8, PORT; 9, WOOD INDUSTRY; 10, SHIPBUILDING YARDS; 11, HOSPITAL; 12, AIRPORT; 13, REST HOMES; 14, PARK OF CULTURE AND REST; 15, WHARVES; 16, SPORT; 17, VOLGA-DON CANAL. IT WAS LATER PROPOSED THAT THE LENGTH OF THE WHOLE BE SHORTENED BY ABOUT 1/4. FROM PARKINS, *TOWN PLANNING IN SOVIET RUSSIA*, FIG. 6.

with brief specifications for the housing unit itself and for the adjoining communal facilities structure. Chapter 10, "Blocking Out the Living Cells and Institutions," illustrates the ways in which several recent architectural projects had combined the residential cells, children's facilities, and communal services. Figures 31–37, which he calls a "single-story corridorless dwelling by Stroikom," are actually taken from Ginzburg's and Barshch's "Green City" project for Moscow, as we have pointed out above in connection with Kaganovich's accusation that Miliutin intended to dismember Moscow. Figures 38–55 illustrate a communal house (*dom-kommuna*), a station, and a club (also from "Green City" but not so labeled). Figures 56–61, called OSA settlement and OSA skyscrapers, are actually from Leonidov's project for Magnitogorsk referred to above. The remainder of the chapter discusses in some detail alternative solutions by the author himself (Figs. 21–23, 65–72). All the projects illustrated in this chapter are in the most advanced International Style of architecture and are organized on linear principles.

Chapter 11 treats various new materials and light mass-produced construction methods—as the author had promised at the beginning of the book. He ridicules the monumentality of and extravagant materials used in buildings designed by conservative Russian architects like Zholtovskii, and to do so cites the same examples that the magazine *SA* had earlier satirized.[55] Chapter 12 continues with the plea for functional modern design; it is copiously illustrated with the works of Gropius, Mies van der Rohe, Hannes Meyer, Le Corbusier, and a Russian team. Miliutin argues: "an honest solution to a correctly stated and correctly resolved problem cannot help but be beautiful." Le Corbusier's Tsentrosoiuz building is pictured (Fig. 92) as is his League of Nations project (expediently labeled "People's Palace"!), in Figs. 90, 91. Miliutin states the position of the Soviet modernist school succinctly and eloquently:

The Soviet settlement must be honest and simple in its forms—as the working class is honest and simple; varied—as life is varied; the parts that make up the buildings should be standardized but not the buildings themselves; economical in the material expended and maintenance but not in their expanse and volume; joyous as nature is joyous. Finally they should be comfortable, light, and hygienic.

The last two chapters are very technical. Chapter 13, "Comparative Costs of Construction," is a demonstration that the use of collectivized services halves the cost of construction of a settlement and brings such facilities within the means of the USSR at that time. Miliutin relies on the data in a recent Gosplan study of the workers' settlement at Magnitogorsk, the tables for which are included in his App. 1. Chapter 14 on the requisite budget for socialized services, and especially education, is exceedingly intricate to follow, but shows that in Moscow, at least, finances are not an obstacle to achieving "socialized education" of children. The rural situation is less sanguine and requires an increase in agricultural production and income in order to pay the costs of schooling. Other collective services —physical ones—can be assumed to be economical by virtue of their large-scale operations. "The form of organization of the dwelling with its subsidiary accommodations is one of the most important elements in the organization of the services for the population," he states, and concludes his book with a quotation from the 1930 resolution of the Bolshevik Party (the whole of which is printed in his App. 2).

Miliutin's Later Writings and the Crisis in Soviet Ideology

In the first issue of his new magazine *Sovetskaia Arkhitektura* in 1931 Miliutin published an article restating certain matters that he had treated in his book, much as if he had in the meantime been questioned on some of his premises and had had second thoughts about their application. His concern was with the problems inherent in the physical and social transformation of housing patterns in order to achieve the new socialist way of life. Following an extensive preamble that reiterated his ideas about the special care necessary to avoid either the extreme of utopianism or that of conservatism during the period of "transition," he summed up in the article a number of conclusions at which he had arrived in his book from Chap. 6 on. He emphasized that although the obsolescent family system could not be disregarded as an institution during the transitional period—especially in rural areas—yet provision should be made in both new buildings and in renovated apartments for the more economically advantageous collective services. He dealt with the setup and linkages of collectivized facilities for the manufacture and distribution of prefabricated foods, with the requisites for nurseries, kindergartens, schools, laundries, repair shops, and cultural centers, as well as with the specifications for the living cell and its furnishings. He also summarized his calculations about the per capita distribution of such socialized services.

His book seems to have been well received. The February 1931 number of the magazine "V.O.K.S." (published by the Soviet Union Society for Cultural Relations with Foreign Countries)—an issue devoted to the place of women in Soviet Russia and the progress of collectivization—printed a slightly abbreviated version of his Chap. 6 under the title "A New Organization of Life." Further official support of his ideas is indicated by a substantial and enthusiastic review of the entire book that appeared in the "New Soviet Literature" section of the same propaganda magazine the following April.

But the clouds were already gathering, and, in 1932 lightning struck the modernist faction of Soviet architects which until then had been riding high.

In a sense, architecture and planning had flourished in relative freedom during the 1920s under a State that accepted the premise that the new revolution of modern architecture corresponded to the revolutionary transformation of the way of life represented by the USSR. In the feverish acceleration towards industrial strength, everyone pitted the Soviet accomplishments in industry and architecture against those of the West and welcomed input from the superior Western technology. There was a strong identification of the modernist architects in Russia with their struggling counterparts in the West. But suddenly about 1932 in a movement that was epitomized, if not run, by Lazar Kaganovich of the Politburo,[56] architectural theory ceased to be concerned primarily with design, construction, and planning problems and became a branch of political theory. By means of an ingenious turnabout argument, modern architecture was declared to be synonymous with bourgeois culture, and tradition was proposed as the basis of Soviet design. Emphasis was on *expressiveness,* not efficiency of function, and the management of traditional city-like agglomerations was to be the thrust of planning—not disurbanization, which had previously been considered to be the more logically proletarian goal.[57] Architectural theory in the Soviet Union was on its way to becoming more of a search for the correct symbolic and aesthetic expression of a particular Party dogma than a discussion of the art and technology of building. As Willen points out, the vocabulary of Marxism-Leninism began to color the discussion, and writers came to depend heavily on quotations from Marxist authorities.

Miliutin had actually been a part of this evolution. Before 1929 and the increasing consolidation of the State as represented by the Five-Year Plan, the identification of the modern movement in architecture and planning with the Bolshevik revolution had been more a general sentiment than a chapter-and-verse philosophical justification. At that point, however, a new cast was given the profession with the formation of VOPRA (the All-Union Society of Proletarian Architects) which, if not actually organized by the Stalinist faction, soon became its vehicle in a search for the architectural symbolism of proletarianism, viz., the pursuit in design of overriding political ends. Dialectics began to buttress architectural precepts. Miliutin's use of quotations from the prophets of socialism was quite effective and was marked by a desire to examine modern ideas of building and planning—mainly Western in origin—in terms of their applicability to the new life in Soviet

Russia; it was devoid of the sophistry that was to make similar quotations after 1932 serve to prove diametrically opposite points. The pressure to shift was apparently irresistible, however, and by 1933 we find Miliutin quoting Lenin as follows:

Marxism has gained for itself the universal historic significance of the ideology of the revolutionary proletariat because Marxism has not thrown away the achievement of the bourgeois epoch, but, on the contrary, has mastered and reworked everything that was valuable in more than two milleniums of human thought and culture.[58]

This idea of Marxism's exploitation of the baggage of the past had already been used by Miliutin in *Sotsgorod*, but now it is being understood as justifying the use of traditional (i.e., classic) architectural styles in the service of the State.

The shift came about inexplicably rapidly. By late 1932 nearly every architect had abandoned and even condemned his earlier modernism. After 1936 there was nothing more to discuss, and apparently no discussions of any substance are to be found in the literature from that date on.[59]

In planning, the big switch of official Party position came at the June 1931 Bolshevik Party Congress to which we have referred above. On that occasion Kaganovich delivered a lengthy discourse on "The Socialist Reconstruction of Moscow and other Cities in the USSR" and submitted a resolution on the subject which was passed by the Plenum.[60] In a sense the message was similar to the resolution of the previous year, which Miliutin reprinted as his App. 2 and took as a theme for his book: disregard futurist and abstract schemes which do not correspond to present possibilities and get down to practical matters at hand. But as opposed to the modernists' plan-theorizing in the USSR, which was what we would today call a "systems approach" and had concentrated on determining the best abstract model, the Soviet capital of Moscow was now assumed as the model, and *ad hoc* procedures of the city-building type that had marked centrist planning since the late nineteenth century were adopted. Kaganovich said:

It should first of all be pointed out that the peculiarity of the question we are discussing consists in the fact that by means of the concrete experience in Moscow we shall solve problems of city development for the whole of the Soviet Union. We are here proceeding from the particular to the general, although, of course, the particular in this case, Moscow, is of decidedly solid proportions.[61]

A stunning reversal. *Sotsgorod*, of course, proceeded from the general to the particular, as we have tried to demonstrate. Fourfifths of Kaganovich's speech was taken up with the "Town Development of Moscow," and, embroidered with anecdote, dealt with admittedly practical matters such as housing, fuel, water supply, road paving, and city transport—all of this in a rather pedestrian and tendentious way.

The assumption is made that in the future Soviet planning would concentrate on urban problems of the traditional sort. Kaganovich a bit later in his speech said:

Yet among us there are pseudo-theoreticians, who, distorting Marx, Engels, and Lenin, consider it our duty to reduce the size of Moscow. Comrade N. A. Miliutin, who works in the Communist Academy, demands that a number of factories and works should be removed from Moscow and its population reduced to 1–1½, or at most to 2 million people.[62]

It is interesting that Miliutin, rather than OSA or Ginzburg, the more radical, should be singled out. A few minutes before Kaganovich had attacked Sabsovich (an extreme *urbanist* who believed in high-density, tightly scheduled city life in what were to be essentially barracks) for Sabsovich's radical collectivism and abolition of the family; he ridiculed Sabsovich's dictum: "There must be no room for the joint habitation of man and wife. . . ."[63] What is apparent is that there was to be no middle ground (where Miliutin stood) and no compromise with either the modernists or (as would prove to be the case) with those with a sympathy for Western advances in architecture such as Miliutin had demonstrated. And, ominously, Miliutin was being attacked for things that he does not really appear to have said.[64] Perhaps it was his substantial position in the Academy and in the Party, and the considerable publicity that the magazine "V.O.K.S." had given his book, that required that he be admonished rather than Ginzburg, who was allowed to continue to talk Constructivism for several years, provided that he did not expect to fill commissions in that style.

In any case, Kaganovich went on to describe how he and Stalin had turned inside out the old Marxist ideal of abolishing the distinction between town and country—especially as it had been understood by Miliutin and other planners of the 1920s:
We are aiming at the abolition of the con-

trast between the town and the country, not by means of the abolition of the town, but by the transformation of the town and the socialist reconstruction of the village, raising the latter to the cultural level of an advanced city. Comrade Stalin, in his speech at the Conference of Marxian Agrarians, pointed out with particular clearness how the question of the abolition of the contrast between the town and the village was to be understood. He said: "The question of the relations between the town and village . . . is assuming a new footing. . . . It will transform the psychology of the peasant and will turn him toward the town. . . . The peasant of the old type, with his barbaric mistrust of the city, which he regards as a plunderer, is passing into the background. His place is being taken by the new peasant, the peasant of the collective farm, who looks toward the city with the hope of obtaining from it real and productive aid.*[65]

This switch to big-city planning procedures (echoing the new traditionalism in architectural design and the re-establishment of pre-Soviet academicians in power) gathered momentum, and the 1932 Bolshevik Party Congress on Moscow sent seven brigades of foreign architects and planners into Greater Moscow to work.[66] Consequently it comes as no surprise that the invitation to the CIAM to meet in Moscow was withdrawn.

In 1932 Miliutin recanted. What he wrote from that time on with regard to architecture and planning represents an about-face that is incomprehensible in terms of Sotsgorod. With two outstanding exceptions, however, all the profession buckled under at about the same time; only

Ginzburg and the Vesnins continued to defend their past.[67]

Miliutin's recantation appeared in his own periodical in the spring of 1932 in an article entitled "Major Problems of the Present Period of Soviet Architecture." While still defending his basic planning concept of linearity on the grounds that it was the product of a study sponsored by the Communist Academy, Miliutin admitted that Sotsgorod suffered from a number of defects. He takes himself to task for having gone along with the disurbanists to the extent that he did on the score of Moscow. He identified those who believed in the theory of disurbanization with the theory of the "immediate withering away of the State" (an analogy which he seems to have taken from Kaganovich[68]). Disurbanization is a "social-fascist" scheme that, under cover of " 'leftist' phrases," spreads the illusion that socialism can be created without the "annihilation of capitalist methods of production" and pretends that the period of the "withering away of the State, of the schools, of the army" has already come; this is an attitude on Miliutin's part that conforms in a way to his earlier preoccupation with the "transitional period." He lashes out at a number of his colleagues, however, labeling the disurbanist Okhitovich of the OSA a "Trotzkyite," while those advocating the urbanist position were "Menshevik-Trotzkyite right-wing opportunists." In general Miliutin began now to reinforce his writings with lengthier excerpts from Stalin's writings, and he becomes increasingly Orwellian in expression. This article certainly contains his most bitter epithets about deviationism.[69]

Miliutin seems to have written nothing more on planning as such but, as an editor and ranking Marxist theorist in the profession, it is of interest to read his later opinions on the subject of modern architecture and its relation to the Soviet situation. In the fall of 1932 he printed the address he gave at the opening of the exhibition of German architecture of that year.[70] He was genuinely enthusiastic to see an exhibit of the works he had so long admired. He cautioned, however, that the programs showed a lack of the social goals that Soviet architects should seek. He praised the "constructivism" of the German work, but warned (and this is the new Soviet line) against excessive formalism on the one hand and unaesthetic engineering on the other. He pointed out that Soviet architecture was striving for social expression and that to do away with such is nihilism: it would be to take the soul out of architecture (in painting, of course, this means "social realism"). Sculpture, ornament, and fresco should not be disdained in the search for a "dialectic unity of all aspects of architecture."

Of the other articles he published during his tenure as editor of the magazine, the most interesting is a series titled "Basic Questions on a Theory of Soviet Architecture"; this is an informally organized and highly personal critique of the art and architecture of the day. It is more a credo of aesthetics than a practical outline of architectural theory.[71]

In these articles he severely criticizes Bekker, a leader of VOPRA, for his assertion that Western ideas should be completely avoided in creating a new Soviet ar-

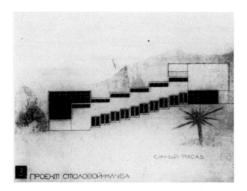

27. N. A. MILIUTIN. PROJECT FOR A DINING CLUB, 1932. FROM *SOVETSKAIA ARKHITEKTURA*, VOL. 2, 1932, NO. 1, PP. 55–56.

chitecture; instead, Miliutin follows Ginzburg's reasoning that there is much of value in European and American architecture that the Russians should utilize. In addition, A. V. Lunacharskii, Miliutin's erstwhile superior in the Commissariat of Public Education, came in for a merciless ribbing for his leanings toward the classical in architecture.

There can be no question of a synthesis of antique architecture (i.e., of the era of slavery) with contemporary forms . . . we want no unprincipled eclecticism such as they have in Washington. . . . Would we equip the Red Army as Greek hoplites?

Or perhaps we could make Doric, Ionic, and Corinthian columns of duraluminum and steel or maybe put a Doric portico over the assembly section of the Stalingrad Tractor Plant. . . .[72]

This comes close to describing the neoclassical excesses of later Soviet architects!

In the course of his "Basic Questions" article, Miliutin brings up the subject of Le Corbusier. His criticism of the Swiss architect seems to reduce to a lament that Le Corbusier was not born a Russian Bolshevik. The fact that Le Corbusier worked under a capitalist system made him the whipping boy for a harangue on economics, rather than the recipient of aesthetic criticism. Miliutin had many times made plain his respect for Le Corbusier's technical accomplishments. His indebtedness to Le Corbusier is reflected in the passage:

We know that life is a constantly developing process and that the eternal in architecture is naive, but this does not mean that we will not have our palaces and monuments as well; but ours will not be like those of Egypt; they will be closer in feeling to Reims and Cluny where all is elastic and moving, where all the elements of architecture combine in amazing unity and clarity of purpose. . . . It is time to stop seeing architecture as something immovable. We build ocean-going architecture for ships and flying architecture for airplanes. Life is movement, too.[73]

Miliutin also uses "Basic Questions" to summarize his views on the history of art, a matter that we can only touch upon here. In

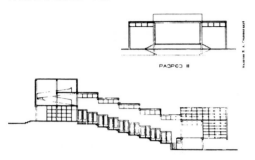

ПРОЕКТ СТОЛОВОИ-КЛУБА

РАЗРЕЗ II

view of his general disparagement of the formalists, we are startled at his lengthy defense of imaginative experimentation in the arts. He argued for more fantasy in creative work and introduced a passage from Lenin's *What's To Be Done?* of 1902, in which Lenin had termed fantasy a "priceless talent." [74] This was particularly intended as a defense of Iakov Chernikhov, the Leningrad Constructivist and professor of architectural rendering. Chernikhov's *Architectural Fantasies*, an exciting collection of 101 colored renderings of visionary architectural complexes, had appeared in 1933, evoking a storm of adverse criticism on the part of other writers. Miliutin illustrates this section of "Basic Questions" with no less than sixteen of Chernikhov's designs and comments upon the "remarkable industrial complex which can be developed into living architecture, made into marvelous paintings or left as inert formalist schemes . . . but the architect who is deprived of fantasy is impotent." [75]

We are further surprised to find him arguing now that modern architecture, and especially Constructivism, represents the decadence of bourgeois society, in particular because of its subjectivism; presumably modern architecture in the USSR was not as subjective because of its social goals, a theme he had stressed at the German exhibition the year before.

Another, later effort that he made to explain the failings of capitalist (Western) modern architecture is an article entitled "Constructivism and Functionalism" in *Arkhitektura SSSR*—so far as is known, his last published article. As Willen observes, he relates the factor of subjectivism in the West ultimately to the enormous profits that big business had made from World War I. Constructivism was a style taken on to beautify the life of the rich and yet not to arouse the "indignation of the working masses." Functionalism, on the other hand, developed in Germany as a result of the economies forced by reparations payments and represented a rationalization of the process that exploited the "toiling masses." Western functionalism's banishment of beauty (which the USSR was now obtaining by its new classicism) represented the decay of capitalism.

As his arguments, like those of so many of his compatriots, became more specious and contradictory he seems simply to have given up, to have stopped writing. There is little to suggest, however, that he ever accepted as completely as others did the new defense of traditional classicism as the vehicle of proletarian ideas. He seems always to have clung somewhat to the earlier direction and method of "transforming the way of life."

We should add that in the pages of *Sovetskaia Arkhitektura* Miliutin published two projects for buildings designed by himself (Pls. 27–29). [76] These are projects for a dining club and a standardized nursery building. The former, shown in Pl. 27, is more or less Constructivist in design, consisting of a series of connected rectangular units set into a hillside. Miliutin here stresses the use of new and inexpensive materials—as in *Sotsgorod*—and the avoidance of applied decoration.

His plan for a nursery (Pls. 28, 29) de-

28. N. A. MILIUTIN. NURSERY PROJECT, 1932. FROM
SOVETSKAIA ARKHITEKTURA, VOL. 2, 1932, NO.
5–6, P. 81.

29. N. A. MILIUTIN. NURSERY PROJECT. FROM
SOVETSKAIA ARKHITEKTURA, VOL. 2, 1932, NO.
5–6, PP. 94–95.

mands the proper choice of color, and
notes the importance of considering the
psychological impact of architectural forms
upon children. The facade, for example,
should present

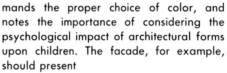

*a contrast of simple planes using the
Golden Section in simple rectangular elements . . . the rhythm of these elements
(columns, windows, frames, etc.) should
range from* adagio *to* moderato *depending
on the physiological and psychological age
of the child.*[77]

The reference to rhythm of architectural elements may relate to Ginzburg's theoretical
work, *Rhythm in Architecture*, while the emphasis upon color most probably stems
from the theories of Chernikhov, for whom
color was the subject of extensive study.[78]

By way of conclusion, what was the impact of Miliutin's book?

Miliutin's influence in Russia is difficult to assess. Although he had some basic and immediate effect on the Party line, it must be assumed that the neoclassic reaction of the thirties effectively suppressed any of his more advanced theories, including that of linear planning. After 1934, to open *Sotsgorod* and be confronted by full-page photographs of Le Corbusier's projects or such renderings as Mies van der Rohe's glass tower was enough to put most architects and students on guard even if they had got by the white square on black which served as end paper for the book and was a motif clearly appropriated from Kazimir Malevich's Suprematist paintings. There is no evidence that any industrial combine in the USSR was laid out according to Miliutin's principles in his day.

His influence in the West seems to have been twofold. Most perceptible is the influence upon Le Corbusier, who in *The Radiant City* demonstrated a fascination with the concept of the "living cell," who obviously relied on Miliutin for his own later *cité linéaire industrielle,* and possibly for some of the segregated functions in the CIAM Athens Charter for which Le Corbusier considered himself largely responsible.

Otherwise Miliutin's Stalingrad plan became almost emblematic of linearism in planning, and it has appeared, as we have noted, in nearly all books on twentieth-century planning theory. It was at first cited as a curiosity, but since linear planning has become such a fad among architects in the 1960s, its influence promises to increase. A similar delayed reaction is now occurring within the Soviet Union. The Khrushchev thaw and the Russian publications that have been permitted to appear on the 1920s, along with the substantial publications abroad, will probably bring Miliutin's *Problem of Building Socialist Cities* into a prominence in Russia that it was not fated to know when it first appeared in 1930.

As Arthur Sprague wrote shortly after his return from an extended stay in the USSR studying these matters:

At this writing, some thirteen years after Stalin's death, the attitude of the Communist Party toward the work of this pioneer of Soviet architecture and planning appears to be changing markedly. The neglect of such figures as Miliutin, Leonidov, and others still unknown to the West has had a deleterious effect on building, both in the USSR and abroad, since dogma and censorship have prohibited any discussion of these earlier experiments in formulating new methods. The spontaneous and imaginative response of intelligent thinkers like Miliutin to the vast problems of building a new society, provoked by the First Five-Year Plan nearly forty years ago, could again today contribute ideas about the building of new cities.

●

THE FOLLOWING NOTES ARE PRINTED HERE AS THEY APPEARED IN ARTHUR SPRAGUE'S M.A. ESSAY ON MILIUTIN: 5, 7, 9, 10, 12, 13, 15, 18–22, 28, 30–33, 42, 50, 53, 69, 75, 76–78. THE FOLLOWING SPRAGUE NOTES WERE MODIFIED FOR USE HERE: 6, 8, 14, 24, 29, 52. (THEY ARE, OF COURSE, NUMBERED DIFFERENTLY IN HIS ESSAY.)—G. R. C.

NOTES TO INTRODUCTION

1. The excitement of this couple of years is most clearly felt, perhaps, in the essay and anthology of Soviet documents published by Paolo Ceccarelli under the title *La costruzione della città sovietica 1929–31* (1970). Among materials included by Ceccarelli are texts of three of Miliutin's chapters, of the resolution of the May 1930 Party Plenum, and of two projects in *SA* (1930) from which Miliutin took a number of his illustrations. This anthology has been translated into Spanish and published by Editorial Gili, Barcelona, in 1972 as No. 9 in the series "Colección Ciencia Urbanística."

2. Le Corbusier's amusing and vivid, but not always accurate comments about the Soviet architecture and his experiences there can be conveniently consulted in his *Radiant City* of 1935 (see pp. 9, 45–47, 74, 84, 90–91, 143–46, 182–83, 288–91 of the Orion Press edition of 1967). The intervention of foreigners in the USSR is detailed in Manfredo Tafuri, et al., *Socialismo, città, architettura URSS 1917–1937; il contributo degli architetti europei* (1971).

3. *Eyes on Russia* (1931). Bourke-White's Chap. XXI is about Traktorstroi at Stalingrad (1929–30), in connection with which Miliutin's famous plan was devised.

4. Ernst May, leader of one of the major German teams in the USSR (or "brigades" as they were called), reported in *Das Neue Russland* (No. 8-9, 1931) that "Material concerning this and other forms of the Socialist City may be found in a book by Miliutin entitled *The Problem of Building Socialist Cities* to be published soon in German translation." Hans Kampfmeyer, who summarized the book in *Bauen und Wohnen* (IV, No. 1-2, 1932) did so from the manuscript of a German translation prepared by an architect-engineer by the name of Grossmann for publication by Rowohlt in Berlin. Ernst May announced in *Das Neue Russland* for Feb. 1932 that the book was actually in press with Rowohlt, but it never appeared, presumably because of the increasingly antagonistic political climate in Germany. A brief summary by the architect Boris Martens was printed in *Die Form* (No. 5, 15 May 1932). The editor of *Die Form*, Ludwig Hilberseimer, was apparently given a copy of Miliutin's book by Martens, and it is from this copy (since disappeared) that the present translation was prepared. The book is frequently cited by Martens' German title for it (see Kopp, *Town and Revolution*, pp. 184, 265), although there is no sign of a German translation ever having gotten into print. Le Corbusier, apparently without seeing it, described the book as "a working contribution to the Five-Year Plan," in *Plans* (July 1931, reprinted in his *Radiant City*, p. 144).

For many years only fragments of the book seem to have been translated into any other language, which is why the present project was launched circa 1960. The frequent comments to be found in the literature on Miliutin and his book were second-hand for the most part and, hence, inaccurate in various ways. Those portions of the book that had appeared in translation by the late 1960s are listed in our translation-notes nos. 18, 36a, 73, 75. As the present volume went into production, word was received of the publication of an Italian translation: N. A. Miljutin, *Socgorod: Il problema dell'edificazione delle città socialiste*, translated by Maria Fabris, with Introduction by Vieri Quilici, Milan, il Saggiatore, 1971. This is, ironically enough, in the same series "Struttura e forma urbana" in which the present editor has published a volume on Arturo Soria and the Ciudad Lineal. It is a straightforward translation with brief introduction about events of the time that does not treat directly of Miliutin and his situation; Miliutin's illustrations are reproduced, but in normal book format with no effort to retain the character of the original. Unfortunately the explanatory Foreword by Meshcheriakov is omitted. This Italian translation was then translated into Spanish, omitting Quilici's introduction and all illustrations except the eight important plans in Chap. 5. The Spanish translation forms part of an anthology which also contains (in Spanish) Ebenezer Howard's *Garden Cities of Tomorrow* of 1902 with its diagrams, Tony Garnier's *la cité industrielle* of 1917 with a few illustrations, sixty-nine illustrations of projects by Ludwig Hilberseimer, and the second edition of Carlo Aymonino, *Origini e sviluppo della città moderna* (Padua, Marsilio Editore, 1971). The Spanish volume appears under Aymonino's name and title with the other translations treated as appendixes and is No. 11 (1972) of the Gili series cited in our note 1 above. Both the Italian and Spanish volumes had to be secured from abroad in order to examine them.

5. A book that reflects, both in its graphics and in its terse prose, the fervor that the First Five-Year Plan generated is M. Il'in, *New Russia's Primer: the Story of the Five Year Plan*, as translated by Counts and Lodge in 1931 (see Bibl.). Chapter XIII, "New People," reminiscent of Edward Bellamy's *Looking Backward*, mentions new cities, communal dwellings, etc.; the first section of this chapter is entitled, "A Fragment from a Book to be Written Fifty Years Hence."

The publication of this book was arranged by Counts, a professor at Teachers College of Columbia University, as an example of the dramatic typography and high excitement used to introduce Russian schoolchildren of 12–14 years of age to the notion of a planned economy and to the subject of social planning. The photographs of the Russian original, laid out somewhat similarly to *Sotsgorod*, were converted into dramatic line-cuts in the style of Rockwell Kent by the unknown designer of the American edition. The British artist William Kermode effected a similar and even more striking transformation of the Russian illustrations for the London edition which also boasted an especially Lissitzky-like binding. But the most remarkable thing is that the following year (1932) the Soviets brought out a mini-edition (pocket-sized) of the Counts translation with the American illustrations and with a complete, phonetically annotated vocabulary section at the rear so that by means of studying the translation of their Primer of the Five-Year Plan, Russian schoolchildren could learn the English language! A film which glorified the Five-Year Plan was made at about this same time by the great Soviet director, Sergei Eisenstein, and is titled *Old and New* (Sovkino, Moscow). This was a remake of Eisenstein's earlier *General Line*. It is of interest that the architectural settings for the film were credited to Andrei Burov, a member of the OSA group.

6. This account is taken almost word for word from the first chapter of Arthur Sprague's M.A. essay on Miliutin. For a general survey and partial bibliography, see Maurice Frank Parkins, *Town Planning in Soviet Russia* (1953). The book is deficient in material regarding the years that concern us and it presents a somewhat romanticized account, drawn largely from sources which were available to Parkins in this country. Miliutin's book is not cited, although his plan is. Information about, and bibliographical material on, the Constructivists is scanty.

Soviet accounts, such as I. G. Sushkevich, *Planirovka i Stroitel'stvo Gorodov SSSR* (*Planning and Building of Cities of the USSR*, 1939), and Vol. XI of the official history by Grabar' of Russian and Soviet art, architecture, and planning, the monumental *Istoriia Russkogo Iskusstva* (*History of Russian Art*, XI, 1957), are highly tendentious and omit many items of real interest. A very brief version of Soviet planning from the socialist viewpoint is to be found in Emmanuel Hruška, *Rasvitie Gradostroitel'stva* (*The Development of Town Planning*, 1963). In short, no accurate or complete coverage exists in any language.

An analytical discussion of recent literature in Russia and the West is to be found in S. Frederick Starr, "Writings from the 1960s on the Modern Movement in Russia" (1971).

7. St. Petersburg was renamed Petrograd in 1917; renamed again in 1924—Leningrad. The capital was transferred to Moscow on 19 February 1918 by Lenin.

8. The law, dated 13 January 1918, read in part: "Private ownership of land and property is to be abrogated; all land holdings are to be declared the property of the whole nation and handed over to the working classes without compensation on the basis of equitable land use. All forests, mineral wealth, and water resources of national importance, all movable as well as immovable inventory, model farm holdings as well as specialized business establishments are to be

declared national property." From P. Martell, "Die Gesetzgebung über das Wohnungsowesen in Sowjet-Russlund" in *Wohnungswirtschaft*, XXIII, 1928, p. 140. Reprinted in El Lissitzky, *Russia*, p. 160. Elaborations of the law are cited in Kopp, pp. 34–36.

See also K. N. Afanas'ev, and V. E. Khazanova, *Iz Istorii Sovetskoi Arkhitektury: 1917–1925* (*From the History of Soviet Architecture: 1917–1925* (1963), p. 7. This is a very general account of early Soviet architecture, but is useful because it contains a number of projects which were not discussed during the repression of the Stalin period of neoclassicism. See also Parkins, pp. 11 and 12.

9. Aleksei Viktorovich Shchusev (1873–1949), architect and city planner, was a graduate of the Imperial Academy of Art in 1897. He was a specialist in ancient Russian architecture and its restoration. A rather pedestrian academician, Shchusev was very influential. He designed Lenin's Mausoleum in Red Square and Liubianka Prison, and founded the Shchusev Museum of Architecture in Moscow.

Ivan Vladislavovich Zholtovskii (b. 1867), teacher and architect, was a graduate of the Imperial Academy of Art in 1896; following this he traveled widely. In Italy he studied Renaissance architecture, in which he became a specialist. In 1936 he translated Palladio into Russian. Zholtovskii was a leader in the neoclassicism of the later 1930s and he designed the well-known Dom na Mokhovoi (House on Mokhovaia Street), first the US Embassy building, and now Intourist headquarters. Miliutin condemned his Gosbank building (Fig. 75) (see Translation, note 60).

10. For illustrations of the first Soviet plan for Moscow, see Grabar', XI, Figs. 138 and 139, and description on p. 137.

11. Some of the obstacles to the achievement of consistent rational planning procedures are described in Martell's article cited in note 8. Kaganovich, in his Party Plenum Address of 1931, which is discussed elsewhere in our Intro-

duction, pointed out that town planning had lagged because "the Party devoted all its energies to the increase of the basic resources of industry, to the rapid development of industrialization, and to agricultural collectivization . . ." (Kaganovich, *Socialist Reconstruction of Moscow and Other Cities in the USSR*, p. 12).

12. See M. A. Il'in, *Vesniny* (*The Vesnins*) (1960), p. 184. This is an interesting account of the work of the Vesnin brothers in architecture both before and after the 1917 Revolution. Drawings for the Burnaev Chemical Plant and for the cement factory at Koktebel are on file in the archives of the Scientific Research Museum of the Academy of Architecture and Construction of the USSR, now located in the former Pervushinskii Church of the Donskoi Monastery in Moscow.

Le Corbusier termed A. Vesnin "le père du Constructivisme Russe"; quoted by Il'in, *Vesniny*, p. 31. V. Vesnin became president of the Soviet Academy of Architecture in the later thirties, a position he held until his death in 1950.

See also A. G. Chianiakov, *Brat'ia Vesniny*, Moscow, 1970.

13. About the Shatursk Power Station, see Parkins, p. 13; it is illustrated in Il'in, *Vesniny*, p. 39.

14. See Parkins, p. 5. Referring to pre-1917 housing, the *Soviet Encyclopedia* says: "The erection of cheap tenement houses by private companies, partly of a semiwelfare character, mitigated the housing distress but slightly." (*Bol'shaia Sovetskaia Entsiklopediia*, hereinafter referred to as *BSE* (1938), XXXIII, p. 653.)

All accounts are full of the miserable conditions under which Russian workers had existed in comparison with their counterparts in the West. See Hans Schmidt and Hannes Meyer, *Schweizer Staedtebauer bei den Sowjets* [1932].

Ceccarelli, pp. ix–xv, goes into the problem of urban immigration during the late nineteenth century and during the early Soviet period in considerable detail, with statistical tables.

15. Afanas'ev and Khazanova, p. 119. An earlier, isolated proposal for a garden city was that included in Roslavlev's somewhat radial plan for Krestovskii Island in the Neva River, a part of the city of Leningrad, in 1917–1919. (*Ibid.*, p. 67.)

16. *Ibid.*, p. 120. Raymond Unwin's *Town Planning in Practice*, a basic handbook of garden city building cast in the German picturesque (Sittesque) manner, was made available in Russia in these years.

Recent literature on the pre-Soviet sources for Soviet planning and on the garden city plans is summarized in Starr, pp. 173–74, and the early garden city efforts in Russia are described in his "The Revival and Schism of Urban Planning in Twentieth Century Russia" in Michael Hamm, ed., *The City in Russian History*, in press (University of Kentucky Press).

17. The plan for the 1923 Exhibition is dated by Afanas'ev and Khazanova (p. 175) as "no earlier than 24 Nov. 1922 to the beginning of Jan. 1923." The original plan is in the Museum of the Revolution of the USSR, Moscow. For this and related plans discussed here, see also, N. P. Bylinkin et al., *Istoriia Sovetskoi Arkhitektury: 1917–1958* (*History of Soviet Architecture: 1917–1958*) (1962), a "history" that is, however, highly pretentious and misleading with respect to the material of the earlier period.

18. Illustrated in enlarged form in Afanas'ev and Khazanova, Fig. 224, p. 176.

19. Il'ia Aleksandrovich Golosov (1883–1945) was a member, apparently, first of ASNOVA and later of OSA (see Glossary). Golosov, in 1929, designed what was probably the best workers' club to be produced by the Constructivists, the Zuev Club on Lesnaia Street. By 1934, however, he was a theorist for classicism, and before long was capable of writing the following: "The intrinsic features of the architecture of the capital of the USSR are bright idioms and light but majestic forms. The elements of classical architecture are used in organic synthesis with

the themes of the Socialist era. This principle will be brilliantly materialized in the Palace of the Soviets, the great monument to Lenin to be erected in the center of Moscow. (*Soviet Cities New and Renewed*, Moscow, Foreign Languages Publishing House, 1939, p. 19.)

20. Afanas'ev and Khazanova, p. 48.

21. *Izvestiia*, 17 and 20 October 1925.

22. For information on the St. Petersburg laws of 1816–40, see Henry Russell Hitchcock, *Architecture: Nineteenth and Twentieth Centuries* (Baltimore, Pelican Books, 1963), p. 58.

23. Kaganovich, p. 84.

24. Kamillo Zitte, *Gorodskoe stroitel'stvo s tochki zreniia ego khudozhestvennykh printsipov* (*City Planning according to its Artistic Principles*) (1925). The Russian translation is discussed in George R. Collins and Christiane Crasemann Collins, *Camillo Sitte and the Birth of Modern City Planning* (1965), pp. 60–63, which includes Arthur Sprague's translation of Mamatov's Preface.

Mamatov seems to have been a perceptive person as regards city-planning procedures, and his Preface to the translation gives a good idea of the uncoordinated nature of planning practice in the USSR before the First Five-Year Plan.

It is a matter of pure conjecture as to how much the ideas of Sitte affected actual construction in Moscow. Evidence would suggest that it was minimal: thoroughfares like Marx Prospect (formerly Mokhovaia Street) in the 1920s, and Gor'kii Street (formerly Tverskaia Iamskaia Street) in the 1930s, were drastically widened to ensure flow of traffic downtown, certainly not in conformity with Sitte. The resulting demolition was on a Haussmannian scale, which greatly appealed to Frank Lloyd Wright when he visited the USSR in 1937, and which he described in his "Architecture and Life in the USSR," *Architectural Record*, LXXXII, No. 4, Oct. 1937, pp. 59–63. He seems to have been particularly delighted with the spectacle of old landmarks being blown sky-high. Traffic now flows through downtown Moscow at a considerable pace.

The clearest instance of an interest in Sitte comes later, in the period of reaction of the 1930s. In *Arkhitektura SSSR* for 1934 (No. 2, pp. 10ff.) under the general title "Gorodskoi Ploshchadi" ("City Squares") a number of authors, including I. V. Zholtovskii and A. Bunin, discussed plaza design, with Sittesque illustrations from Padua, Pisa, Rome, and Pompeii. Willen (p. 187) is of the opinion that this influenced the design of Moscow's new squares.

25. For a report on these recent items, including exhibitions, see Starr.

26. Le Corbusier, *Radiant City*, p. 145.

27. He seems to have had a particular grudge against Lunacharskii, the Commissar of "Enlightenment," who had in 1928 awarded the prize for the Lenin Library to Shchuko, an academician, for a classicistic design—over two modernists, Markov and the Vesnins. Early on in his book (Chap. 2) Miliutin ridiculed his ideas about city building, and he did so again in 1933 after Lunacharskii had become spokesman for the classical cause. Lunacharskii strongly disapproved of Le Corbusier's Tsentrosoiuz building.

28. See R. Khiger, "M. Ia. Ginzburg," for further biographical details of Ginzburg.

29. Most thorough and pertinent analysis of the book is in Willen. An earlier text by Ginzburg, *Ritm v Arkhitekture* (*Rhythm in Architecture*) (1923), which treated the rhythmic repetition of architectural forms, preceded *Style and Epoch*. *Rhythm in Architecture* was written during a brief period of collaboration between Ginzburg and Shchusev, while the former was associated with MAO. A journal (*Arkitektura*) was edited jointly by the two men, but only two issues appeared (1923). Due to differences of opinion, Ginzburg resigned and went on, along with the Vesnins, to found OSA.

30. Dom Narodnogo Komissariata Finansov (House of the People's Commissariat of Finance), known as "Dom Parokhod" ("Ship House"). Ginzburg usually collaborated. In this case he was assisted on the preliminary project by G. A. Zundblat (see Fig. 76) and on the final construction by I. F. Milinis.

31. Domnarkomfin contained some 100 units and was built on pilotis (now filled in to form a ground floor). It was also provided with connecting kindergarten, cafeteria, and laundry. The complimentary description of it by M. Il'in in the first year of "V.O.K.S." (1930) is interesting by way of contrast with the architectural reaction that was so soon to set in:

"Out of the many apartment houses of the same general [newer] architectural style, the house for the employees of the People's Commissariat of Finance which has been designed by Ginsburg [Ginzburg] and is now nearing completion is particularly worthy of notice. Although this group is not strictly speaking a commune, many of its activities have been organised on a communal basis, and consequently the house merits special attention. It is a five-storied house divided off into small apartments in such a manner that two corridors are sufficient for the entire house. The interior plan of the apartments has been drawn up with an eye to making cheerful pleasant homes, and with the greatest possible economy of space. Every detail of each room is worked out so as to be in keeping with the other rooms and in harmony with the central plan. The continuous windows, the manner in which each apartment [duplex] is laid out on two floors, and the shape of the rooms join in creating a joyous and cheerful atmosphere in the whole house. The same impression is maintained throughout the entire building the front view of which is so shaped as to suggest, to a certain extent, an ocean liner." It is unclear whether the author was Mikhail Andreevich Il'in or Il'in Iakovlevich Marshak writing under his pseudonym (See Bibl., Il'in, M.).

The relationship of this building to Le Corbusier's idea of a Unité de Habitation is obvious. A concise statement about the relevance of Western developments and Le Corbusier's concepts in particular to the Soviet situation appeared in an article by Ginzburg "The International Front of Contemporary Architecture" a couple of years previously.

32. See *BSE* (1954), XXVII, p. 494, for details of Miliutin's activities as a bureaucrat, including his work in insurance, hospital administration, and on various government committees. His activities as a revolutionary are stressed in this brief biography and in foreign-language ones dependent upon it, but his function as a planner and author of *Sotsgorod* is not mentioned, as we have noted. See his early bibliography.

33. Leonard Schapiro, *The Communist Party of the Soviet Union* (1960), p. 343. For an extended discussion of the establishment and activities of the Communist Academy, see "V.O.K.S.", IV, No. 5, (1933), pp. 28–36.

34. Georges Benoit Lévy, the French garden city and linear city advocate, considered Miliutin to be the Russian representative of his International Association of Linear Cities during the 1930s; in his annual reports for 1934–35 and 1936–37 he described communications received from Miliutin. A brief report by Miliutin on the iconographic program followed for the artistic decoration of the Palace of the Soviets in 1939 is to be found in the publication of that date listed in his bibliography.

35. *Town and Revolution*, p. 115. An electrical condenser does not actually transform the nature of a current, of course, but it does produce a mysterious surge that perhaps justifies the use of the simile.

36. Miliutin's essential humanity was such that we do not find in his book the glib and patronizing references to the working class that mark the exhortations of figures like Kaganovich. An interesting discussion of mythologies about the working class and its function in a revolutionary society can be found in a series of contributions entitled "Communism: 125 Years Later," on the *New York Times* "Op-Ed" page

during July, August, and December 1972.

37. The term "cell" is here employed in the Russian text not for the feeling of incarceration that it implies in English, but rather to reflect the marriage of form and function, such as is found in the cells of biological systems. Martin Wagner, the Berlin planner, commented in *Tagebuch XXX* for 25 July 1931: "The basic life cell of the Socialist City is the individual dwelling unit." (Reprinted in El Lissitzky, *Russia*, p. 212.) Le Corbusier was enthusiastic about the concept and prepared a memorandum for the 1930 Brussels Congress of the CIAM entitled, "The Biological Unit: The Cell of 14 m² per Occupant" which he published in *Plans* for 1931 and in *The Radiant City*, pp. 143–46. He discussed Miliutin and Ginzburg in the memorandum and considered his living cell, supported by air-conditioning, to be superior to the Russian 9 m² models.

38. See Kopp, *passim*, and Ceccarelli, *passim*.

39. In this connection, the recent article by Frampton, "Notes on Soviet Urbanism, 1917–32," is inaccurate in identifying Miliutin as a left-wing planner and influential disurbanist. In fact the author attributes greater specific impact and action to Miliutin as a planner in Soviet Russia than we know him to have had. As we try to make clear here, Miliutin's schematic plans were abstract models for the purpose of comparison and criticism in a study by the Communist Academy—not actual layouts. The vagaries of contemporary reports about the planning controversies in the Soviet Union and the general inaccessibility of Miliutin's book have led writers even to characterize him as an *urbanist!*

40. See Parkins, p. 28.

41. El Lissitzky published a contemporary Russian linear plan as well as the Spanish diagrammatic linear plan (Pl. 22) in his *Russland* of 1930. He mistakenly attributed the latter to the French economist Charles Gide who was an influential propagandist for Arturo Soria's *Ciudad Lineal.*

42. The conception of architecture as machine had long before this penetrated Soviet thinking, and examples of an *architecture parlante* are numerous. In 1927, for example, in the competition for the Lenin Library, one design—that of W. Pashkov—was in the form of an oil-fired boiler, while an even more interesting one—that of Ivan Il'ich Leonidov (1902–60)—symbolized Lenin's emphasis upon electrification and the "rise" of Soviet society with a building which carried reference to both the light bulb and the aerostat (Pl. 12).

See Werner Hegemann, "Lenin Ehrung: Auditorium Glübirne oder Luftballon?" ("Lenin's Monument: Auditorium, Light Bulb, or Balloon?"), *Wasmuths Monatshefte*, XIII, 1929, pp. 129–132. For Pashkov's project see Conrads and Sperlich, *The Architecture of Fantasy*, p. 96.

43. For his reduction of this to the principle of the conveyor belt, see p. 73.

44. Although on this very page (see p. 51) he has a footnote exempting from criticism the use of skyscrapers (presumably à la Le Corbusier or his friend Ginzburg) that clear the ground for greenery in urban renewal. Ernst May reported on the general Russian rejection of the American skyscraper (included in El Lissitzky, *Russia*, p. 174).

45. This is a translation of "potochno-funktsional'naia sistema," p. 23 of the Russian text (see p. 65 of the present work).

46. The tractor was the heroic emblem par excellence of Russian five-year planning. This mechanized draft animal (Le Corbusier termed it "Le cheval sans pattes et sans vétérinaire.") summed up the aspirations of the collectivization and industrialization of agriculture and man. Along with the hovering dirigible and dramatic perspectives of the Dnieper Dam, it monopolized the design of posters, postage stamps, and propaganda magazines of the day. The very first issue of "*V.O.K.S.*" (I, 1930, p. 16) described how the Red Putilov, a former munition works in Leningrad, purchased a single Fordson tractor

in 1924, redesigned it, and by 1929 was turning out thousands per year of the improved model—which was then being studied by Ford's engineers. The plant, incidentally, memorialized the small lathe at which M. I. Kalinin, President of the Soviet Union, once had worked.

Nevins and Hill, pp. 674, 676, 678, 682, reported that the Putilov tractor was a rather poor copy of the real Fordson, that it was produced in considerably less quantity, and was sold by the government at half its actual cost.

47. Margaret Bourke-White reported on the Stalingrad crash program:

"From other sources, I discovered other aspects of Tractorstroi [*Traktorstroi*]: Tractorstroi holds the construction record in the Soviet Union. It was built in one year. The original plan was to have the plant completed in 1931 or 1932, but it was finished in 1930 and in June of that year the first tractor came off the conveyor. The construction of this plant illustrates the role played by American firms having technical assistance contracts in the Soviet Union. On May 8, 1929, a Russian commission from Tractorstroi visited the Detroit offices of Albert Kahn, Inc., and outlined the first instructions regarding the design of the plant. The firm of Albert Kahn started to make the architectural and engineering plans for the construction on May 10; the preliminary studies were approved on May 20, and the construction drawings were started the following day. Because the Russians were anxious to complete the plant as soon as possible, Albert Kahn put a large force of experts on these construction drawings and completed them by July first. The firm then sent six American specialists to Stalingrad to supervise the erection of the plant.

"Actual construction was started on July 16, 1929. All the structural steel for the plant was purchased in the United States. The speed with which 5,700 tons of steel were erected into a framework constitutes a record in Russia, all the more remarkable in view of the fact that the work was done by Russian laborers with little previous experience in this kind of construction. The entire plant was substantially completed on February 28th, 1930, about seven and one-half months after starting, a record, which, in view of the magnitude of the project, would have been good even in the United States. The total cost of the plant was about $36,000,000, which does not include the cost of the apartment houses, stores, schools, theaters, and other buildings in Stalingrad constructed around the plant for the convenience of the workers.

About 6,200 workers were engaged in the construction of the plant, which consists of ten principal buildings and a half-dozen auxiliary buildings. All the buildings are single-story structures, designed to embody the latest American ideas of factory construction. The mechanical equipment of the buildings is also principally American. The Russians, as well as the firm of Albert Kahn, are proud of the fact that only one year after construction was started the first tractor was delivered, despite the fact that a large part of the building materials and practically all the mechanical equipment had to be obtained abroad, and that the workers employed in the manufacture of tractors were untrained and all had to be broken into their various duties." (Bourke-White, *Eyes on Russia*, pp. 123–24.)

A list of the Kahn projects in the Soviet Union is to be found in A. Kahn, Inc., *Industrial and Commercial Buildings*, Detroit, Architectural Book Publishing Co., 1937, Appendix.

48. VSNKh made a special contractual arrangement with Kahn to provide architects and engineers for industrial development in the USSR, of which the Stalingrad plant was the first result; see A. L. Drabkin, "American Architects and Engineers in Russia" (1930). Drabkin was a principle designer of the plant, which was supposed to produce 50,000 tractors a year.

49. This factory, designed to produce Model A Ford cars and Model AA and larger

trucks, was the largest assembly plant in the world after River Rouge. It was started early in 1930 and was to be producing on 1 January 1932. The project and the building campaign were reported with great interest in the *New York Times Magazine* of 9 August 1931 (a feature story written by Allen R. Austin, whose engineering firm did the installation). Follow-ups appeared in the *Times* financial pages of 29 November (p. 19) and 2 December (p. 45) 1931. The general plan and housing settlements were of a form initiated by Ernst May's brigade; they are illustrated in Tafuri, Figs. 50–51.

50. Henry Ford, *Mein Leben und Werk*, Leipzig, P. List, 1923.

51. Joel Kovel in the *New York Times Book Review*, 14 February 1971, p. 5.

52. It is not without interest to note the individuals from whom Miliutin quotes, both in this book and in general. In *Sotsgorod* there are 11 quotations from Marx (or Marx and Engels); 8 from Engels solely; 8 from Lenin; 5 from Stalin. He also quotes from Syrtsov and Lunacharskii (Soviets) and from Barbon, Goethe, and Pushkin. In his other writings he quotes from or refers to the following: Aristophanes, Aristotle, Virgil, Hegel, Schiller, Rousseau, Balzac, Flaubert, Swift, Delacroix, Sholem Aleichem, and Somerset Maugham.

Marx was quoted by Miliutin chiefly on abolishing the distinction between urban and rural life, on the matter of education being combined with productive work, and—by way of the famous passage from the *Manifesto* (with Engels)—on the family. Engels was cited by Miliutin on the same subjects and also on getting rid of the "big cities." Lenin he quoted twice, emphatically, on the redistribution of mankind and also about the emancipation of women. Miliutin quoted Stalin several times, apparently out of a sense of duty, because Stalin's words added little or nothing to the argument, unless it be a certain sense of urgency.

53. See Ernst May, "Cities of the Future."

For an account of the complex history of Magnitogorsk, see G. B. Minervin, ed., *Magnitogorsk* (1961) (from which our illustration of the state of the plan in 1933 is taken).

The wholesale departure of Ernst May and his staff from Frankfurt to Soviet Russia in 1930 was an epical event. The accomplishments of May in housing at Frankfurt had been matched only by the new workers' housing in Berlin, and in 1929 he had hosted the second CIAM meeting (on low-income housing). He was largely responsible for the intrusion into Russia of the German *Zeilenbau* layout of apartment buildings running perpendicular (like a comb) to their streets, and his reports from Siberia and his lecture-visits back home are among our most valuable sources of information about what was actually going on in the USSR in those years. Apart from May, the best known Germans active in the Soviet Union were probably Hannes Meyer and Bruno Taut.

54. Ernst May also had submitted a project for Stalingrad, a linear one organized like Fig. 13, according to his account of Soviet planning in *Das Neue Russland* in 1931. He faulted Miliutin's proposal because "It ignores the important function of the Volga as a transportation element, for the river provides a cheap and natural means of delivery and dispatch of raw materials and finished products to and from the industrial plants that make up the 35-km-long linear city."

55. *SA*, II, 1927, No. 2, pp. 47–50.

56. Willen notes that Kaganovich looms large in official accounts of Soviet architecture, citing as common the following reference in an editorial in *Akademiia Arkhitektury* (1934, No. 1, p. 4): "Under the talented and concrete leadership of Comrade Kaganovich, the architectural collective of our land has achieved significant successes in the fulfillment of the directives of Comrade Stalin on architecture." (Willen, p. 140.)

57. Willen, whose unpublished study is still the most sensitive analysis of the architectural

situation, shows how the new theory used the arguments of one modern faction (the formalists or rightists of ASNOVA) to demolish those of the other (the constructivists or leftists of OSA) and vice versa, and then proposed a resolution of the matter (but not a mean or intermediate) in the recourse to tradition. Lunacharskii, whom Miliutin apparently already disliked, supplied the key exposition of this, and Kaganovich seemingly masterminded the campaign. Willen suggests similarities to the way in which, earlier, Stalin played off Trotsky and Bukharin, one against the other, and then took over. Donald Egbert's analysis of the politico-cultural situation regarding Stalin, Bukharin, and Trotsky substantiates this (*Social Radicalism and the Arts*, NYC, Knopf, 1970, p. 293). One can get the flavor of the matter from Kaganovich's 1931 Bolshevik Party Plenum Address in which he ended up his analysis of Soviet town planning goals by attributing to those who held theories contrary to his the following labels: Menshevik Trotskyism, recrudescent Trotskyism, right deviationism, stagnant conciliationism, the rights and lefts and conciliationist opportunist groupings (Kaganovich, pp. 103–4).

58. *Sovetskaia Arkhitektura*, III, 1933, No. 5, p. 21. Willen's translation.

59. Willen devotes his last chapter to this phenomenon, but assures the reader that architects were not liquidated; no trials or punishments are known.

60. Both are to be found in Kaganovich.

61. *Ibid.*, p. 61.

62. *Ibid.*, p. 97.

63. *Ibid.*, p. 87.

64. Miliutin was opposed to unplanned concentration in cities and had cited Moscow as an example of this. He had not said explicitly that Moscow should be decentralized, but he did print, under another title, the "Green City" proposal for doing just that. Also he did identify cities with capitalism, their dispersion with Marxism, and he questioned the value of tinkering with existing cities—which was just what Ka-

ganovich was proposing to do. Also, Kaganovich may for his part have misunderstood Miliutin's intentions. It was not a matter of reducing the number of residents in Moscow, but rather—as Miliutin maintained in various places in his book—that a lower urban population would be sufficient to provide the requisite labor force because a greater percentage of residents would be employed, owing to the advantage of collectivized services.

65. Kaganovich, pp. 98–99. Curiously enough, when major extracts of the Kaganovich speech were distributed to the world via "V.O.K.S." (II, No. 5-6 of May-June 1932) neither the criticism of Miliutin nor of Sabsovich was included, and the purpose of the speech becomes ambiguous, sounding more like Miliutin's middle position. A following article on "New Soviet Cities" by S. Gornyi takes over a number of Miliutin's basic precepts and speaks of the Communist Academy's study of city planning—again remaining curiously vague about what precise forms were to be followed.

66. This activity is described by Schmidt and Meyer in *Schweizer Staedtebauer bei den Sowjets* [1932].

67. The rapidity of this change of attitude and its relation to the takeover of the architectural profession by the State apparatus is documented step by step in Willen's study. Many of the figures whom we have mentioned or Miliutin discussed (Lunacharskii, Zholtovskii, Ginzburg, the Vesnins, Kaganovich) play leading roles in Willen's chronicle, which should be made more generally available for students of the field.

68. In the same passage in which he had criticized Miliutin, Kaganovich said: "It does not need to be shown that talk of the withering away, the self-abolition and the reduction of cities is sheer nonsense. Indeed, it is harmful. It is as though one were to discuss the withering away and abolition of the State as a practical question of the present day. Here, of course, there is a definite analogy. . . . We know that a

time will come when the State will wither away; yet today we keep on strengthening it, we are concentrating into a single fist all the forces of the proletarian State for the struggle against the class enemies that surround us. . . ." (Kaganovich, p. 98)

This position is developed comprehensively in latter-day Marxist terms by F. Svetlov and S. Gornyi in their "The socialist city in a society without classes" of 1934. They attack the radical urbanists, the radical disurbanists (especially Okhitovich), and also Miliutin whom they consider to be a disurbanist designer of bourgeois suburbs the sole purpose of which (like Ernst May's satellite towns) is the exploitation of the working proletariat with no thought for their mental well-being in beautiful surroundings. They quote from many of the resolutions that Miliutin did, but use them differently. Gornyi seems to have been something of a hatchetman; he had ridiculed Le Corbusier's Tsentrosoiuz in 1930 and labeled Ginzburg's *Housing* of 1934 as petit bourgeois.

69. N. A. Miliutin, "Vazhneishie zadachi sovremennogo etapa Sovetskoi arkhitektury" ("Major problems of the present period of Soviet architecture") (1932). This was reprinted in *Bol'shevik* of the same year. His invective in this article is some of the most extreme that he ever wrote, for example: "Down with the feudal, kulak, Trotskyite . . . cubo-futurist bastards!"

(For the content of some of these later articles by Miliutin, after 1931, I have relied on the Masters essays of Sprague and Willen, not having read all the originals myself—G. R. C.)

70. *Sovetskaia Arkhitektura*, II, No. 3-6, Sept.-Dec. 1932, pp. 17–18.

71. "Osnovnye voprosy teorii Sovetskoi arkhitektury" ("Basic questions on a theory of Soviet architecture") (1933).

72. *Sovetskaia Arkhitektura*, II, No. 2-3, 1932, p. 7; No. 3, 1933, p. 11.

73. *Ibid.*, No. 3, 1933, p. 7.

74. *Ibid.*, No. 3, 1933, pp. 5–6.

75. *Ibid.*, No. 3, 1933, pp. 5–6. See Iakov Chernikhov, *Arkhitekturnye Fantazii (Architectural Fantasies)* (1933); Arthur Sprague, "Chernikhov and Constructivism" (1961). Chernikhov's designs and writing (translated by Sprague) are in Conrads and Sperlich, *The Architecture of Fantasy* (1962), passim.

76. N. A. Miliutin, "Proekt kurortnoi stolovoi klub" ("Project for a Resort Dining Club") (1932); "Iasli" ("Nurseries") (1932).

77. *Ibid.* The drawings for both the nursery and dining-club projects were done by Sergei Egorovich Chernyshev (b. 1881). From 1934 to 1941 Chernyshev was chief architect of the city of Moscow. See Grabar'.

78. See, for example, Iakov Chernikhov, *Bazy Sovremennoi Arkhitektury (Bases of Contemporary Architecture)* (1930).

N. A. MILIUTIN

THE PROBLEM

OF BUILDING

SOCIALIST

CITIES[1]

BASIC QUESTIONS REGARDING
THE RATIONAL PLANNING AND
BUILDING OF SETTLEMENTS
IN THE USSR.

STATE PUBLISHING HOUSE
MOSCOW LENINGRAD 1930

Н. А. МИЛЮТИН

ПРОБЛЕМА СТРОИтельства СОЦиалистических ГОРОДов

ОСНОВНЫЕ ВОПРОСЫ
РАЦИОНАЛЛЬНОЙ ПЛАНИРОВКИ
И СТРОИТЕЛЬСТВА
НАСЕЛЕННЫХ МЕСТ СССР

ГОСУДАРСТВЕННОЕ ИЗДАТЕЛЬСТВО
МОСКВА ● ЛЕНИНГРАД 1930

I DEDICATE THIS BOOK TO THAT MOST PRACTICAL OF ENTHUSIASTS, **A. P. SMIRNOV.**[2]

N. MILIUTIN

FOREWORD

The unprecedented rapidity with which our country is being industrialized presents us with the question of creating new large-scale manufacturing centers, as well as the necessity for intensified construction in those industrial cities that already exist. Each year these problems become sharper and more pressing in direct proportion to the accelerated tempo of our industrialization.

However, in order to solve these questions of construction, we cannot travel along the old, well-worn paths of pre-Revolutionary Russia—paths which are still being followed in capitalist countries. We cannot build according to those archaic methods which are inescapable where there is no single planned social economy, where every owner of a factory or apartment house can build wherever he fancies and however he chooses. Our socialist building cannot and must not repeat all the mistakes and absurdities of the past. A more **rational** construction of industrial enterprises and their contiguous residential areas is possible: that is the problem that faces us and

for which, in solving, the outmoded methods and old plans are almost completely futile.

But there is another factor that makes the old model unacceptable for us. In a capitalist society apartment houses are produced either in the interests of those wealthy persons who, having put up a building exclusively for themselves, then live there luxuriously, taking up gigantic spaces with their small families and arranging the house to their own capricious taste—or else it is built in the interests of those landlords who break it up into apartments and cruelly exploit the tenants. In such houses all the interests of tenants and all questions of their comfort are sacrificed to the greed of the landlord-exploiters. Our constructions must be carried out only in the interests of the working people who are to live in them.

Finally, the ever-increasing drive toward collectivization of life impels us to build houses in an entirely different way than they have been up to this time and as they are still constructed in capitalist countries, where the basic economic unit is the family, each with its individual economy.

All this brings us to realize that these questions of new city building have become unusually acute in the last year. During the winter of 1929–30, they were frequently and heatedly discussed in a number of speeches and papers before various societies and institutions. At the present time one notices everywhere tremendous interest in these questions. In the future this interest will grow even more in proportion to the building of our cities and dwellings.

Unfortunately we have hardly any literature on this subject. It is almost entirely limited to short articles in newspapers and magazines. It is, therefore, a great pleasure to welcome new books on the subject, especially when the author treats the problem from a position of real knowledge of the matter.

The present volume is of this category. The author, N. A. Miliutin, has extensive knowledge of the subject, since he is the chairman of the government commission on the construction of new cities.

N. A. Miliutin's book is distinguished by two advantageous circumstances:

1. Many writers, discussing questions of contemporary construction in the USSR, confuse two issues: the building of dwellings at the present time (a period of transition to socialism or of the beginning of socialism) and the planning to be done at a more distant date in the period of a fully developed socialist or even communist society. This leads them into two kinds of errors. On the one hand, they do not take into account the great progress in techniques and transportation which will have been made in the future, but instead carry over into the future the same handicaps which we so keenly experience in the present; as a result of this their picture of the future assumes a dim and miserable character (for example, they retain in the socialist era the same crowded living conditions in dwellings which we, due to insufficient means, have to accept in the present). On the other hand, in planning both for the present day and the near future, they make demands that cannot be fully realized at present (for example, the immediate and complete collectivi-

zation of life, the elimination of the family, etc.). Comrade Miliutin's book does not suffer from these drawbacks. He says nothing about the far distant future. He is only interested in those questions of constructions that are before us **at the present time.** "In order to establish new principles for the residential sectors of Soviet settlements **for our transitional epoch,**" he writes, "we must first enunciate clearly those problems which will present themselves **in the immediate years ahead.**" This clear distinction between the building of the near and distant futures saves Miliutin from a number of the mistakes of those visionary and fantastic projects of which many have been guilty in their discussions on the subject of planning during this past winter 1929–30.

2. The second outstanding feature of N. A. Miliutin's book is the author's solid knowledge of the subject at hand. He presents the questions under discussion not in a general way, not as bare theoretical plans, but practically, accompanying his presentation with a number of examples and plans taken from actual life. This aspect further enhances the interest and usefulness of the volume.

In view of all this, one must warmly recommend N. A. Miliutin's book to all who desire to familiarize themselves with the issue of our new building, with the problems that it involves, and with the devices and resources which may bring about its practical realization.

N. Meshcheriakov[3]

FROM THE AUTHOR

▬▬▬▬▬▬▬▬▬▬▬▬▬▬▬▬▬

This book by no means pretends to offer an exhaustive solution to all problems concerned in the planning of settlements in the USSR. We have set ourselves the task of formulating in specific terms only those requirements of Soviet construction that result from the analysis of K. Marx, F. Engels, and V. I. Lenin. We must carefully evaluate the basic technical and material capabilities which we have at our disposal at present and make, if only in outline form, some first concrete decisions about dwellings for the workers in this first stage of socialism.

In making our decisions we have tried to adhere strictly to the method of Marxist analysis, keeping constantly in mind the basic (overall) problems that face us, and the specific social relationships, the level of technology, and the availability of materials under present conditions in the USSR.

To solve many questions we found it necessary to examine all available publications on new achievements in the technol-
ogy of construction, and also to analyze carefully the ideas of outstanding architects including the Constructivists (in particular, the works of Le Corbusier, Gropius, Ginzburg, Vesnin, Leonidov, et al.). We have also had to examine a considerable number (more than 50) competition entries on the construction of socialist cities as worked out by both Soviet and foreign architects.

In addition, the author, as chairman of the government commission on the planning of socialist cities, has become intimately acquainted with all basic literature on the subject and has heard out a number of opinions and discussions of it from the most diverse points of view.

Finally, we have become familiar in particular with a number of works and studies by Gosplan, Narkomzdrav, and Narkompros, which deal with aspects of the problem.

If what we are introducing in this work has any originality, it is due only to the extreme paucity in our country of serious works on questions of the new way of life and the new architecture.

This same situation has involved us in carrying out for our book a number of special works, involving the designing of projects, programs and plans for buildings, and tables of statistics (see Figs. 11, 14, 16, 21–23, 65–72).

During the preparation of this book we became firmly convinced of the necessity for creating a special experimental institute for urban design which, if properly organized, could represent a saving of many millions of rubles annually.

DESIRE IMPLIES WANT. N. BARBON [4]

The massive reconstruction of the economy on socialist principles inexorably demands a reconstruction in culture and in our way of life. Appreciable numbers of workers and peasants even now are not satisfied with the existing conditions of life. Our daily struggle to root out the remains of capitalism in the economy and the great successes that we have attained in this pursuit have opened the eyes of wide masses of the laboring class to the abominations of the petty bourgeois way of life, for **"after the revolution, millions of people will learn more in a week than in an ordinary year of the old somnolent life." (Lenin)**

The reconstruction of our way of life on new socialist principles is the next problem facing the Soviet Union.

Along with this, we are confronted with the overall problem of sanitary and health improvements in settlements throughout the USSR; nor can we allow the kind of criminal anarchy in construction procedures that characterizes the capitalist world. The Soviet village must be built in such a way as not to perpetuate the very conditions we are struggling against, but rather to create the basis for organization of a new socialist, collective way of life.

The millions of rubles we spend on our housing and socialist construction must serve the cause of inculcating the new way of life, i.e., the socialist system for the care of cultural and living conditions among the population, which is a necessary precondition to the freeing of women from

1 THE ESSENCE OF THE PROBLEM

In the light of the Five-Year Plan and, therefore, even more so for those of longer range, the problem of construction of settlements in the USSR takes on an exceptional significance. The fate of billions of rubles for new construction depends on how and what we decide to build. Suffice it to say that in the current Five-Year Plan, as much as 15 to 20 billion rubles are required for even one nonindustrial construction.

Hundreds of new settlements are being created; vast construction is taking place in existing cities; the construction of agricultural cities [*agrogoroda*] as a nucleus for large-scale state farms [*sovkhozy*] and for the complete collectivization of entire districts and provinces is being considered.

DIALECTICS TREATS THINGS AND THEIR INTELLECTUAL REFLECTIONS, MOST IMPORTANTLY IN THEIR INTERRELATIONSHIPS, THEIR LINKAGE, THEIR MOVEMENT, THEIR EMERGENCE AND DISAPPEARANCES.   F. ENGELS

domestic slavery. This problem is perfectly stated by V. I. Lenin in the following words:

Woman continues to remain a domestic slave in spite of all our liberating laws, for she is weighed down, smothered, stupified, and humiliated by petty domestic tasks which chain her to the kitchen and to her nurseries, rob her of her effectiveness by viciously wasteful, cheap, nerve-wracking, strangling, stultifying work. The real liberation of woman, the real communism, will begin only when and where begins the struggle (led by the proletariat which derives its power from the State) against this petty domestic economy or, more accurately, with a massive restructuring of our economy into a large-scale socialist one.

In the meantime, we are not only building dwellings according to the old merchants' concept, but even the construction of our cities goes on most often according to old-fashioned (traditional) methods. The distinguishing features of this type of construction are: the small family apartment, designed for individual maintenance in all respects, and the historical city laid out around a central market.

The most characteristic example of this type of construction is our own capital, Moscow, where, in spite of the tremendous wastes involved, we have not built anything basically new and where until now all construction still gravitates toward Kitaigorod, i.e., the ancient market.[6]

The attempt to depart from these forms of city building by erecting skyscrapers is basically a mechanical copying of the usual capitalist forms of residential arrangement. The skyscrapers are the peak —the last cry of capitalism. Interspersed throughout the city, they change nothing in its way of life, in the edification of the masses, or in production. The skyscraper both expresses and finalizes the idea of capitalist centralization, deriving as it does from the concentration of trade and production in large centers. These centers spring up independently of the presence of natural resources or of power facilities, because capitalist cities have popped up primarily as a function of the position of a market or trade route and not at all in connection with the productive process.●

All these principles of the anarcho-capitalist system of city building must be decisively repudiated as being in no way related to the problems of reconstructing our economy and to the way of life based on socialist principles.

We must shrug off this "historical legacy" unequivocally.

It should be all the more easy for us to do this since the fund for municipalization (i.e., the assets at the disposal of the city and village soviets) is at present about 11 billion rubles. In view of the tens of billions of rubles, which, due to new planning principles, will be available in the next few years, it is evident that any other course would be criminal sabotage, not only in considering future generations but so that present-day youth, too, can leave behind the rotten old stoves and dusty beds of their grandfathers' era.

Finally, the exceptionally high cost to us of building houses and communities forces us to seek a radical cutting of costs by changing a number of deeply ingrained principles (actually prejudices) in our construction methods. Without solving this problem we will be unable to eliminate overcrowding, one of the most serious obstacles in the cause of socialist construction and in the reconstruction of our way of life.

"The organization of the advance of socialism on all fronts" (J. Stalin) must also signify an advance in the struggle for a new and healthy life for the working classes.

●

● It must be mentioned, however, that one should not make a general indictment of the skyscraper as a form of construction, since there are those instances where it is expedient that it be used as a means of freeing the ground for the planting of greenery, etc., in extant cities that are under reconstruction, viz., in the changeover to new principles.

THE TASK CONSISTS OF THE NECESSITY OF CONTINUING AN IMPLACABLE STRUGGLE ON TWO FRONTS.
J. STALIN, SPEECH AT THE XVI PARTY CONGRESS [7]

2 THE AVOIDANCE OF EXTREMES

It would be groundless and foolish for us today to solve the problem of our settlements by thinking of them as future residential areas under fully developed socialism. We have now neither the technology nor the material means that will be developed in the future to do this. It is only necessary to glance back at the utopian socialist settlements of the middle ages to see that they reflect precisely the economic and social conditions as well as the technological conditions in which men lived at that time. Thus, one of the great utopians in the sixteenth century thought of the socialist city as a fortified city, beginning a new era in which young people (!) could take a bath once a month (!) and change their underlinen! [9]

Things are no better in contemporary attempts to describe the city of the future. As A. V. Lunacharskii writes in *Revolution and Culture*, No. 1, 1930:[10]

Thus the general character of the socialist city will present itself as a disciplined unit of great diversity. In the center of the main square (we are discussing a typical city) will be concentrated all the buildings in which is located the real heart of the entire city [!]. Here will be the greatest monumentality [!], the greatest variety of forms. This will be the architectural center-of-gravity of the city. From here in radii [!] and rings [!] will be arranged the wide streets [!] perhaps interrupted from time to time [!] by gardens, boulevards, special squares, pools of water, fountains, etc. From it [the center— A. S.] will spread these communal dwelling houses, also monumental [!], built in such a way as to clearly, but [!] with variety, divide its internal essence, i.e., that arrangement whereby the industrial living quarters will be arranged around their grouped individual hearts [!]: their cultural clubs and other such general quarters.

In this excerpt in which the author summarizes his article about "The architectural character of socialist cities," it is easy to see that even as exceptionally talented and up-to-date a person as A. V. Lunacharskii, in attempting to construct an architectural

IN THIS MATTER, AS IN A GREAT MANY OTHERS, THERE IS UNDER THE PRESENT CIRCUMSTANCES A DOUBLE DANGER. ON THE ONE HAND THERE IS A SLUGGISH AND CONSERVATIVE RESISTANCE TO EACH FRESH THOUGHT AND IDEA ON THE PART OF THE REPRESENTATIVES OF MORE CONSERVATIVE TENDENCIES WITHIN OUR APPARATUS. ON THE OTHER HAND, THERE CAN BE DISTRACTIONS AND PROPOSALS WHICH IN THE GIVEN SITUATION ARE UNREAL AND FANTASTIC.
S. I. SYRTSOV, SPEECH AT A CONFERENCE ON THE QUESTION OF THE CONSTRUCTION OF SOCIALIST CITIES, 11 FEBRUARY 1930 [8]

plan for the future socialist city, was prisoner of the aristocratic Russian Empire, with its individual "hearts," "monumentality," "rings and radii," etc.

We will leave it to the novelists to draw the pictures of the city of the future under developed socialism. Today, in the words of Goethe, "it is as much a secret for fools as for sages." [11] Today we are interested in our contemporary construction **on the basis of contemporary technology and the material means presently at our disposal**. We must keep in mind that the problem of "overtaking and surpassing" the capitalist countries is one of strengthening the defense capabilities of a proletarian state that is surrounded by an inimical capitalist world—and a problem of making over both our industry and our agriculture. These problems force us to limit in every way possible those resources that might otherwise be used to satisfy consumer demands.

From this it inevitably follows that in trying by all possible means to solve the problems of building a new way of life and to achieve new forms for the construction of settlements, we must seek those procedures which will allow of a solution to these problems without any proportional increase in expenditures.

Along with this, we must start from the prevailing wage level of the workers. It would be possible to come up with a lovely plan for a socialist dwelling unit which in actuality would be completely impractical and unrealistic since it would in no way correspond to the standard of living available to us today.

In this way the problem of building socialist settlements today is primarily reduced to the root and basically new rationalization of constructing and reconstructing our way of life on the basis of those material means which are at our disposal at the present time.

However, this in no sense means that we must reconcile ourselves to an animal level of dwelling existence in which wallows the major part of the working class of the rest of the world and a significant proportion of the workers of the USSR. Any such interpretation of our current problems must be refuted with the same resolve we would use to meet any other reactionary postures. **"The establishment of socialism in our country cannot help but entail the systematic betterment of the material condition of the workers." (J. Stalin)**. The masses of workers and peasants must see that the dictatorship of the proletariat not only opens before them the broadest perspectives into the future but also brings a real, actual raising of the standard of living and of the level of culture, and reinvigorates and reconditions the tenor of their life. Any different solution to this question (as once expounded by certain Trotskyites) would be, objectively speaking (i.e., regardless of what one wished) a reactionary one.

While raising the tempo of accumulation in the country (capital investments in agriculture) we must simultaneously raise the living standard of the laborer. The basis for this should be the increase in labor productivity and the socialist rebuilding of our economy and way of life.

In this way and only in this way can the question of the establishment of a new social milieu in the USSR be resolved. ●

ANY SOCIAL REVOLUTION MUST TAKE THINGS AS IT FINDS THEM AND IMMEDIATELY ELIMINATE THE MOST GLARING ABUSES.   F. ENGELS

3 URBANIZATION OR DISURBANIZATION?

In the western press today and among outstanding modern architects, a lively discussion is going on: should cities be built according to principles of concentration (centralization) of industry and trade at a few points (urbanization) or—the other way round—should it be done by dispersing industry and residential areas over as wide a territory (area) as possible by building small settlements and separating the living quarters from the industry ("garden cities," "green cities," etc.)?

The partisans of one or the other point of view, as a general rule, proceed from an idea that is based on economic relationships which they accept as being immutable. The bourgeois architect can, of course, see things no other way.

For him there is only the irrefutable premise of the capitalist system and its laws, with its reckless exploitation of the proletariat, its disregard for the most elementary needs of the laboring masses, and its brutish standard of living.

The terrifying living conditions of workers in capitalist countries, where they are deprived even of light and air and where their children spend their lives in dirty back yards near garbage dumps, give rise, among the better bourgeois architects, to the liberals' ideas of "green cities," "garden cities," etc.

However, we understand perfectly well that these ideas, in spite of all their alluring qualities, are a pure and, what's more, evil utopia, creating the illusion (false representation) of a possible escape from the situation without doing away with the capitalist system. These illusions blunt the proletarian's will to fight. Capitalism gives the workers just enough to keep them from dying from starvation. The capitalist is not interested in how long a worker can survive under these barbaric life conditions into which he is driven; the reserve army of the unemployed is always at his service. "Disurbanization" is unthinkable under the capitalist system.

Urbanists, aware of the impossibility of disurbanization under capitalism, try to find a solution to the problem of reinvigorating life by means of technological services within the big cities. Sewer systems, water works, multilevel streets, green areas and similar nice things—that is the way of the urbanists.

However, life itself turns their schemes

1. **THE NIGHTMARES OF THE "MODERN" METROPOLIS.** LONDON.

inside out in its own way. The reinvigorated quarters, as Engels already noted, are not actually lived in by the proletariat, because their life denies them the means to afford it.

These controversies between the urbanists and disurbanists are also reflected here, assuming at times rather amusing forms.[12]

We must, however, phrase the whole problem differently. The question of restricted land for big cities is inapplicable here since we have destroyed private ownership of the land.

Any ideas about the necessity for maximum (more rational) use of "communally serviceable" areas is simply comical, since no such areas exist here.

But most important **is the tremendous problem of the elimination of the differences between the city and the country.**

This is why **we must review the very meaning of the word "city."**

The modern city is a product of a mercantile society and will die together with it, merging into the socialist industrialized countryside. The problem has been presented by V. I. Lenin in the following way:

[The problem is] *the unification of industry with agriculture on the basis of a conscious application of science, the combination of collective labor and a new distribution of mankind (with the elimination of rural desolation, its isolation from the rest of the world, its wildness, as well as the unnatural crowding of enormous masses into big cities).*[13]

2. ⟵ **NEW YORK** ⟶ 3.

4. A CORNER OF PARIS.

Karl Marx, in his Manifesto of the Communist Party, formulates this problem in this way:

The combination of agriculture with manufacturing industries, the gradual abolition of the distinction between town and country.[15]

Finally, F. Engels, in his exceptionally valuable book, *The Housing Question*,[16] says:

There is no sense in trying to solve the housing question by trying to preserve our big cities. The elimination of the difference between the city and the country is no more nor less utopian than the elimination of the difference between the capitalist and the hired worker. Each day it comes nearer being a practical necessity for both industrial and agricultural economy. . . . Only as uniform a distribution of the population as possible over the whole country, only an integral connection between industrial and agricultural production together with the thereby necessary extension of the means of communication—presupposing the abolition of the capitalist mode of production—would be able to tear the rural population out of the isolation and stupor in which it has vegetated for millenia. It is not utopian to declare that the complete emancipation of humanity from the chains which its historic past has forged will only be complete when the antithesis between the town and country has been abolished; the utopia begins only when someone undertakes from existing relationships (Engels has in view, of course, the capitalist conditions.—N. M.) *to prescribe the form in which this or any other antithesis of present day society* (capitalist.—N. M.) *is to be solved.*

In this way, socialist settlements will differ markedly from that which we see today in our city or countryside: they will be neither the one nor the other.

For us there can be no controversy about urbanization or disurbanization. We will have to settle the problem of the new redistribution of humanity after we have eliminated that senseless (for us) centralization of industrial production which gives birth to the modern city.

With the elimination of centralization (concentration) of production the notion of the centralization of habitation (the city) falls away, and consequently so do ideas about "garden cities," etc.

On the other hand, we will do away with the extreme isolation of the country, which engenders the isolation and wildness of the rural population. This elimination, again, will ensue not from our settling the argument about the "principle" of urbanization, but from the mechanization of agriculture, which inevitably leads to its strengthening and to a certain amount of concentration.

The city and the town stretch out their hands to one another: thus will these arguments be solved.

6. HELL ON EARTH

THE IMAGE OF CONTEMPORARY CAPITALIST INDUSTRY

CIVILIZATION HAS LEFT US THE LEGACY OF HUGE CITIES, AND TO GET RID OF THEM WILL COST US MUCH IN TIME AND EFFORT. BUT IT WILL BE NECESSARY TO GET RID OF THEM, AND THIS WILL BE DONE.   F. ENGELS

4 CHOOSING SITES FOR NEW CONSTRUCTION

Existing cities were created in the interests of the ruling classes, the enemies of the proletariat. These cities sprang up on the basis of trade capital and were laid out on trade routes which, in most instances, have lost their function today. As a result, existing cities, as a rule, are not particularly related to natural resources of raw materials and to centers of power. Industrial construction in these cities derived least of all from the interests of their population; instead it has concentrated around markets which have also lost their previous significance. There was, of course, no question of planning. In choosing sites for new construction, we are forced to reject categorically the mechanical following of tradition in the selection of administrative, industrial, and other such centers. We must proceed from an assessment of the economic, political, and natural conditions that give us the most

expedient solution to the building problem in each instance.[17] **This is why our growing tendency to build new installations where there are already existing cities and villages containing similar establishments must definitely be stopped.**

The possibility and necessity of settling this question was shown by V. I. Lenin in the following words:

At the present time, when the transmission of electrical energy over long distances is possible and when the technology of transportation is improved, there are absolutely no technical obstacles to resettling the population more or less evenly over the entire country, and still taking advantage of the treasure houses of science and art which have for centuries accumulated in only a few centers.

Any piling up of separate enterprises at one point, when the processes involved are not directly interconnected, must be immediately curtailed because of its obvious inexpediency.

New construction must be carried out as a unified and economically complete industrial combine which will insure more economic use of raw materials, of waste materials, of accessory energy, etc. In addition, each of these new undertakings must be judiciously coordinated with its residential zones and the corresponding auxiliary commodity sources (dairies, private vegetable and flower gardens, collective farms [*kolkhozy*], state farms [*sovkhozy*], farms [*fermy*], etc.). **In this way, at the basis of** the solution to the problem of the choice of sites for new construction must lie the creation not of industrial and other centers, but of productive-agrarian centers which will be the basis for creating the populated settlement with its corresponding cultural, social, scientific, educational, and other similar institutions and collateral enterprises.

Only with this solution to the question of the choice of sites for new construction will we be able to proceed to the decision of how to redistribute mankind on the basis of socialist production. It must be remembered that if the pivot for capitalist economy is the market and its laws, then the pivot for socialist economy must be production and its planning.

Does it follow from this that the now-existing cities, settlements, etc., as well as routes of communication, must be altogether ignored? Of course not. In a number of cases extant sites will be satisfactory for the conditions we are establishing for socialist production. More than that, the existing means of communication are as needed as the air we breathe. However, it does not follow that they must determine the locations for new construction. The immense investments we are now making in arteries of communication make it possible for us to choose an economically more expedient approach, and this lowers (but does not eliminate) our dependence on extant routes for the choice of new sites. It is highly likely that, with time, the technical development of air communication will put the problem in a new light. However, today, if we do not wish to lose contact altogether with reality and lapse into the visionary, we must in no case drop off into fantasy but keep both feet solidly on the ground.

We cannot throw into the trash basket indiscriminately everything which we have inherited from the past. We must transform and assimilate this heritage in such a way as to have it serve our purpose and not interfere with its realization. We must not forget for one minute that— *the elimination of the differences between the city and the country is one of the first conditions for collectivization* (*K. Marx*).

From this, the conclusion must be drawn that the construction of new enterprises, of scientific and special educational institutions, etc., in existing cities can only be permitted where there exists a direct productive linkage between these new undertakings and those already in existence in the settlement—as well as the presence of raw materials and power supplies. The "pros" and "cons" must be carefully weighed in the choice of the site. One must not repeat those mistakes made when we added to a trifling shop worth from 100,000 to 200,000 rubles, a plant, by way of "reconstruction," that was worth some millions of rubles. In this way we spoiled both the old shop and the new plant.

In any case, expansion of existing settlements, if it turns out to be absolutely necessary, must be done either by creating satellite towns, or by replanning these settlements, or (in extreme instances for particularly large cities) replanning their separate parts. This replanning must be based on those principles by which we build new settlements, i.e., affording maximum dispersion of the population, creating the premises for the organization of a new way of life, improvement of these cities by freeing large areas for the planting of greenery, etc. No matter what happens, we must avoid being strangled by the dead past. It is therefore inadmissible to make significant capital investment in the old cities without formulating a general preparatory scheme for the reconstruction of these cities and settlements.

Only then will we have avoided the great and useless (and, it follows, harmful) wastes of undertaking new construction in old settlements.

A few words about architectural construction. The problem of abolishing the distinction between industrial and agricultural production, as well as the problem of the industrialization of agriculture, is understood by many comrades to signify the installation of a variety of small-scale industrial enterprises within *sovkhozy* and *kolkhozy*.

Putting it this way reveals a misunderstanding of the question. The slogan "industrialization of agriculture" first of all means mechanization of the process, and not propagation of small-scale industry throughout the countryside. All the advantages of large-scale mechanized production (industrial as well as agricultural) must be exploited fully. The combining of the advantages of city and village life must be brought about through a "new distribution of mankind" (Lenin) and not through a propagation of small-scale handicrafts throughout the countryside.

Integration of the production of agricultural raw materials and their processing in a single enterprise must be allowed only in cases where it would be economically expedient (for example, in the sugar and distilling industries, in the initial processing of market-garden products, of milk, etc.).

General conclusions: **in choosing sites for new construction, priority must be given to the interests of the proper organization of production** (both industrial and agricultural), **while taking into account the interests of the population at the same time. We must not follow mechanically the lines of existing cities and transportation arteries, nor must we pile up on one spot a variety of undertakings that are not connected by their industrial processes; we must solve correctly the problem of inter-relating industry and agriculture on the basis of the redistribution of mankind.**

●

HOWEVER WE DEVELOP OUR NATIONAL ECONOMY, WE CANNOT AVOID THE QUESTION OF HOW CORRECTLY TO DISTRIBUTE INDUSTRY [SO THAT IT BECOMES] **THE MAIN ELEMENT OF THE NATIONAL ECONOMY.**
    J. STALIN

5 THE PRINCIPLES OF PLANNING [18]

If we examine a properly planned large-scale, steam-operated electric power station, we see the following picture: directly next to the transportation lines are located the reserve fuel dumps; next in line are the boiler installations, supplied with fuel by elevators, conveyors, etc.; beyond this line of boilers are the machines which transform the steam into mechanical energy; behind these steam engines are placed the dynamos which produce electric energy; further along are the distribution switchboards, beyond them the transformer—and still further, the transmission lines.

By laying out the installation this way, we keep machines of one type in clear-cut lines, thereby greatly shortening all the

transmission and distribution lines for fuel, steam, and energy. Moreover, the system allows for general servicing of analogous installations—by appropriate crews—and of their subsidiary elements such as approach routes, conveyors, air filters, steampipe lines, valves, etc. Finally, thanks to this same system, the expansion of the station is facilitated by means of a corresponding parallel construction of entire aggregates as parts of the whole system.

If such a station were to be built in helter-skelter fashion, that is, according to no system at all, then one can easily imagine what chaos would ensue, with increases in the price of equipment, in maintenance, etc.

It is precisely this chaos, multiplied thousands of times, that we have in contemporary cities. Here we find industry and residential areas located side by side; beyond them, new apartment houses; further on a hospital, another factory; then, somewhere else, a transportation line, more residences, administrative institutions, and so on and so forth. This chaotic condition complicates interurban transportation and increases the cost of communication routes; it complicates the layout of sewer systems and water supplies, dirties the city, poisons the air and the earth. The increased rates of illness and death in the large modern city, the huge and wasteful expense on interurban transportation of freight and passengers, the high cost of communal services, etc.—all

this forces the issue of a radical change in the principles of city planning.

We are led to the same conclusion by even the most cursory acquaintance with today's method of planning towns and population aggregates as a combination of private dwellings and apartment blocks. We must eradicate this system, since it grew out of private ownership of the land—which we have done away with—since it requires an utterly wasteful surveying of each plot, and finally, since it also splits the economy and the territory of the various parts of the settlement, which exceedingly complicates any general solutions.

We must approach each site as a unified whole in which the basic elements are as rationally and expediently distributed as possible; these include industrial and agricultural production, transportation, power, administration, general living conditions, upbringing of children, and education.

Therefore, in the projecting of new settlements or the replanning of existing ones (including their individual parts), the following major objectives must be unconditionally guaranteed:

1. It is absolutely necessary that productive units be rationally united with one another and with major transportation routes. In addition it will be absolutely necessary to consider the most economical flow (the shortest, and where possible, most direct lines ●) in the organization of the processes of production for the entire combine and also in the linkage of the units of production with the communes, with the dwellings, and with the other similar parts of settlements.

A flowing functional-assembly-line system is the absolutely necessary basis for new planning.[20]

2. **The residential sector** (zone) **of the settlement** (the communal, residential, children's, and similar buildings or institutions) **must be set up parallel to the productive zone and must be separated from it by a green belt** (buffer zone). This protective strip must be no less than 500 meters wide, and must be increased depending on local conditions and the character of the production.

Only under these conditions, without the superfluous expense for intersettlement transportation, can we arrive at that point where a worker's home will be situated no more than 10–20 minutes' walk from his machine (place of work) and which will allow him all the advantages of village life (air, forest, fields).

3. **Railroad lines must be laid out behind the production zone, i.e., behind the line of industrial buildings, while the highway should be between the productive and residential zones** (in the green belt). On the one hand, this insures the free deployment of production and transportation lines on the side opposite the residential area of the settlement and, on the other hand, it insures intersettlement communica-

---

• Direct, as is known, implies the shortest and, therefore, the most economical distance between two points. For some reason this elementary axiom has been forgotten by our planners as well as by our technologists.

tion by automobile (buses, etc.). In addition, railroad stations and warehouses will be placed between the railroad lines and highways for the best servicing of the needs of both production areas and the settlement.

4. The most desirable **placement for agricultural territory** (dairy farms, horticultural *sovkhozy*, bee farms, etc.) is out **past the residential areas of the settlement.** This would provide the following advantages: *sovkhoz* workers will live in the same settlement;[21] night soil could be directed to the fields by the shortest possible and greatly simplified means;[22] products would be transported to the residential zone from the railroad stations and warehouses by the shortest possible routes.

5. **The necessary sites for special buildings for secondary and higher technical and agricultural educational institutions must be situated in the area used by the corresponding activity;** and, where applicable, this should also apply to the placement of administrative institutions (with institutions teaching economics close by) and hospitals (with the medical faculties close by), etc.

Such an arrangement simplifies the problem of the rebuilding of educational institutions along the line of their corresponding industry when **"education and labor will be united"** (F. Engels). By the unification of educational institutions with production laboratories, work shops, fields, libraries, archives, etc., we will not only achieve significant economies, but will also make possible the great idea of turning an industry into a school. Every male and female worker (including the cook in factory kitchens, the hospital attendant, the courier

in Soviet institutions, the shepherd on the *sovkhoz*) will have the opportunity to become an engineer, surgeon, economist, agronomist, etc., in the course of his or her usual work.

This prospect of uninterrupted intellectual growth will create such an enthusiasm in the widest sector of the population, such an increase in energy and a will to work and to learn as the capitalist world does not dare even to dream of!

6. **Medical institutions** must be divided into 2 groups: a system of separate dispensaries and of hospitals.

The dispensaries must be situated in the residential zone, but the hospitals must be out toward the border of the settlement in more salutary locales. These latter institutions must be built on the pavilion system and, in addition, must not only be hospital-schools but also polymedical clinics that would include hospitals, sanatoriums, scientific institutes, etc. The expediency of this type of organization cannot be disputed.

7. **School buildings** (for the first seven years) **must be connected with the corresponding children's dormitories,** which, in turn, should be organized along pioneer lines (like camps).

At the same time, **these institutions must be very closely connected to cultural-social institutions** (clubs, libraries, etc.) and production activities. This is the means whereby we will attain the situation—

that will, in the case of every child over a given age, combine productive labor with instruction and gymnastics, not only as one of the methods of adding to the efficiency of production, but as the only method of producing fully developed human beings (**Karl Marx, Kapital**).[23]

At the same time this will enable the interaction between themselves of various generations of the population on the basis of work and culture, since **the present influence of the family on upbringing must be gradually replaced by the influence of the collective.** It is self-evident that any attempt to effect a solution to this problem mechanically must be rejected. However, in the new territorial arrangement for population settlements, we must take this problem fully into account in order **not to hinder life where it is ripening for the development of new forms.**

We must take into account the fact that the tempo of our reconstruction of the economy cannot bypass nor disregard our standard of living. Any attempts at hindrance to this would clearly be reactionary.

8. **Proceeding from the most rational solution to the problem of services for the whole settlement** (or its parts), **communal undertakings** involving production **must be situated in the productive zone.** Moreover, the unity of the communal economy must be unconditionally guaranteed. It would be inadmissible if these enterprises were to solve this problem independent of the community services (the separate fire depots, dining halls, water supplies, etc.).

9. **Warehouses** must also be situated in the productive zone, in immediate proximity to railway terminals or corresponding activities.

10. The consideration must be met that in the future, in step with the construction of new buildings, "all unsound and badly built homes and apartments will be destroyed" (K. Marx–F. Engels, *Communist Manifesto*).[24]

In this way, **the planning of new settlements and the replanning of existing ones amounts to setting up the zones for the future settlement on the basis of a clearly worked out, most economical plan for movement of goods and people, and a layout for the basic linear system.**

These zones should be laid out in the following order:

1) area for railroad lines (segregated band);

2) area (zone) of production and communal enterprises, warehouses, station emplacements, and related scientific, technical, and educational institutions;

3) green belt (buffer zone) with major highway;

4) residential zone where, in turn, will be laid out:

a) a band of social institutions (dining halls, dispensaries, meeting quarters of the town-village soviets,[25] etc.);

b) a band of residential buildings;

c) a children's band, i.e., nurseries, kindergartens, dormitories;[26]

5) park zone with institutions for recreation: ball fields, swimming pools, etc.;

6) zone for garden and dairy *sovkhozy* (irrigated fields, farms, and similar agricultural enterprises).

No alteration in the internal order of these six basic zones of different purpose should be tolerated under any circumstances since it would not only destroy the overall plan but would hamper the development of each part (the growth of the settlement), would create unsanitary living conditions, and would deprive us of those tremendous advantages which the functional-assembly-line system affords.

In determining the layout of the various zones special attention must be paid to extant bodies of water and to the direction of the prevailing winds.

A solution must be sought which would place these **bodies of water** (rivers, lakes, large ponds, etc.) **on the side of the residential zone.** This will not only be an attractive addition to the settlement and will afford a space for parks along their banks for vacation institutions, ball parks, etc., but it also has great sanitary and hygienic significance.[27]

The matter of prevailing winds must be handled **in such a way that prevailing winds blow from the residential side toward the industrial, and not vice versa.**

It is self-evident that when we speak of "lines," "bands," and "zones" of construction, we have in mind not absolutely straight lines but linear zones which are adjusted to the local topography and to convenient communication. It should be noted, however, **that local variations of topography do not play an important role in the layout of most of these zones of settlements.**

In this respect, we are subject to a number of misconceptions. For example, it is usual to think that the site for the construction must necessarily be level, forgetting that there are **numerous productive processes which depend on vertical or inclined flow** (even within the building). It can even be advantageous to place residential and social buildings on hills: for instance, it is convenient to place theatres and auditoriums on an incline. **The eccentricities in the configuration of a site are a help and not an obstacle to a keen engineer and architect.**

The reason for variations in the lines and layout can be: rivers, transportation, swamps, etc.—but not the desire to obtain a smooth surface which no one needs in the first place.

●

7. BUILDING FOR A SUMMER THEATRE IN DNEPROSTROI:
AN EXAMPLE OF THE SUCCESSFUL EXPLOITATION OF LOCAL TOPOGRAPHY.

For purposes of illustration, let us take three plans of Magnitogorsk.

a) **The plan** for Magnitogorsk that **was accepted in competition** (Fig. 8) has the following shortcomings:

1) the factory territory is heaped in one lump; there is nowhere to expand;

2) the railroad lines cut off the factories from the residential areas;

3) the institute of higher learning is separated from the factory;

4) the Soviet institutions are also cut off;

5) the distance to work for half the workers will be more than 3 km, reaching as high as 4 and even 7 for some;

6) the residential area is also heaped in a lump. One cannot even speak about contact with rural life;

7) the water basin (Ural River) is not used at all for the settlement;

8) the streets are overextended due to the rectangular layout;

9) the influence of wind blowing from the factory to the settlement has not been entirely eliminated.

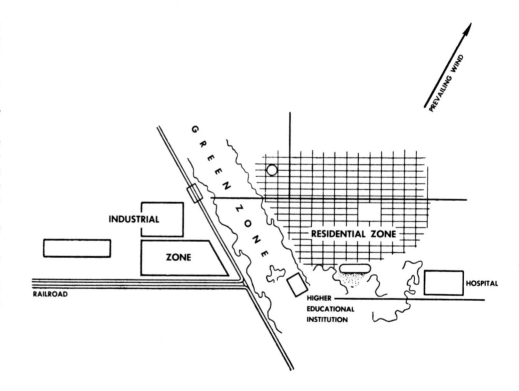

b) **The plan proposed by OSA** (Fig. 9):

1) as regards the planning of the factory and communication routes, this scheme suffers from the same deficiencies as the one accepted in the competition [Fig. 8];

2) the distance to work for the majority of the inhabitants is more than 6 km and reaches 21 km, which means significant wastes in intersettlement transport with probably doubtful results;

3) the residential section is ideally planned, with the exception that the water basin of the Ural River is not utilized.

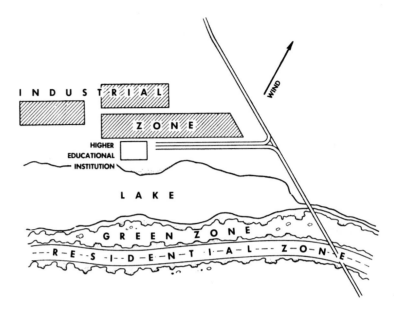

10. **SCHEME** FOR THE PLANNING OF MAGNITOGORSK **PROPOSED BY STROIKOM OF THE RSFSR.**[30]

9. **SCHEME PROPOSED BY OSA** FOR THE PLANNING OF MAGNITOGORSK.[29]

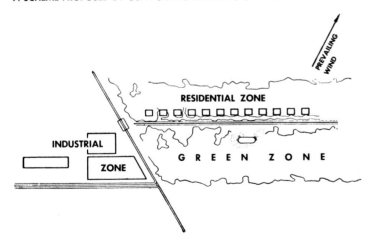

c) **The plan proposed by Stroikom** has two major shortcomings (Fig. 10):

1) the distance to work from the homes is from 2 to 21 km;

2) the water basin is hardly utilized.

In other respects the plan is completely satisfactory.

d) **Our own proposal for a plan according to the functional-assembly-line system** (Fig. 11) is a correction of the plans of OSA and Stroikom, and is devoid of their shortcomings. The longest distance from work is $1\frac{1}{2}$ km, and for most workers it is 500–700 m.

The village is all in greenery and runs along the bank of the Ural, which is dammed to form a lake; special quarters for the technical and higher institutions of learning are near the production centers; the station is in the center of the settlement along with cultural and Soviet institutions. From windows of the residential buildings only the park or the river is visible.

A hospital (laid out in pavilion form) is situated on the bank of the river.

The railroad runs behind the factories and is from 1–2 km away from the residential area.

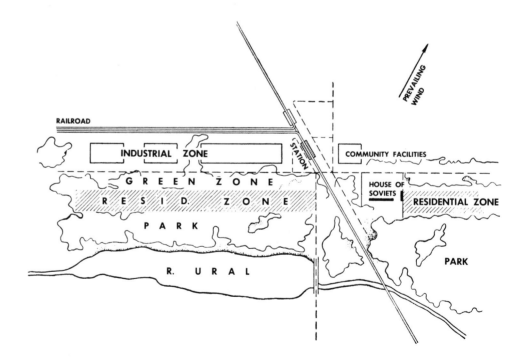

This plan reveals eloquently the advantages of the functional-assembly-line system from all points of view, without exception.

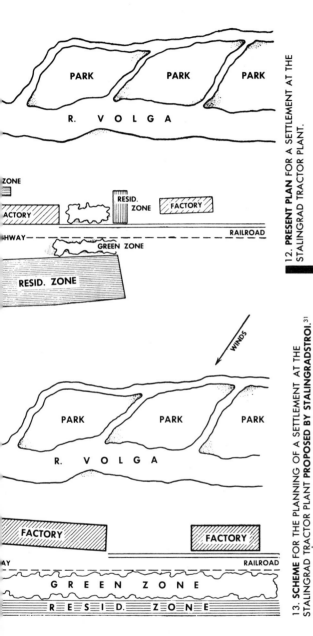

12. **PRESENT PLAN** FOR A SETTLEMENT AT THE STALINGRAD TRACTOR PLANT.

13. **SCHEME** FOR THE PLANNING OF A SETTLEMENT AT THE STALINGRAD TRACTOR PLANT **PROPOSED BY STALINGRADSTROI.**[31]

We see the same situation in the plans for Stalingradtraktorstroi (see Figs. 12–14).

Taking the functional-assembly-line system as our basis for the planning of settlements, we can solve the problem of the most rational and economic arrangement of the transportation. A number of constructions (viaducts, tunnels, approaches, etc.) become entirely unnecessary or can be reduced to a minimum.

Intersettlement transportation is no more the meaningless transportation of endless masses of workers to and from work. It becomes tied to the way of life and, of course, allows a tremendous economy in expenses otherwise wasted on equipment.

14. **SCHEMATIC** FOR THE PLANNING OF A SETTLEMENT AT THE STALINGRAD TRACTOR PLANT **ACCORDING TO THE FUNCTIONAL-ASSEMBLY-LINE METHOD.**

The streetcars could be replaced by a few buses, taxis, and the like. The extension and number of the paved streets in the settlement can be sharply reduced, and these roads assume the appearance of arterial highways.

The water arteries, running the length of the settlement, open new prospects for inexpensive light-tonnage transportation, by both motor and sail boats. Aviation thus receives a "free" navigating beacon in the form of these ribbon settlements which give by their illumination a sharp outline to the map of the area.[32]

In brief, the linear nature of transportation finds its best advocate in this system.

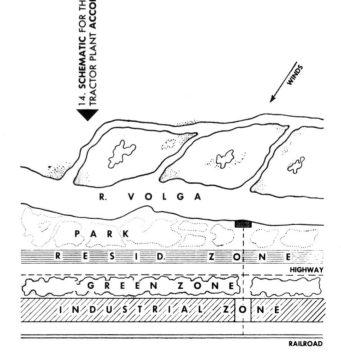

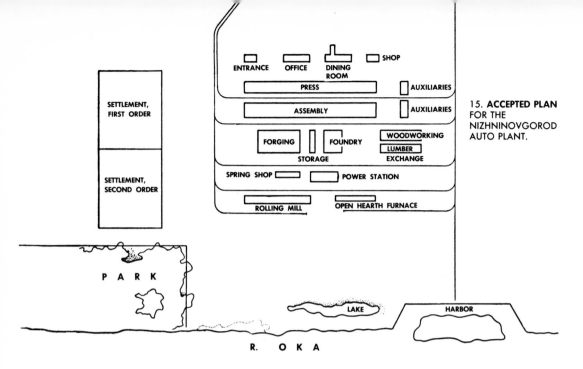

15. ACCEPTED PLAN FOR THE NIZHNINOVGOROD AUTO PLANT.

only swirls about but cuts back into itself. Coal and iron ore going to the open-hearth furnace cross the mechanics' and the pressing areas; metals on the way to the foundry and forge cross the power station; freight is constantly whirling about in circles; personnel go back and forth to the settlement across the railroad tracks. The whole combine will be like Hell itself.

If only the shops were placed in one stream then we would have the following (see Fig. 16).[34]

It is easy to see that all the defects we have mentioned before are here cleared up, automatically, with no added wasteful expenses whatsoever and, on the contrary, with significant reductions in expense—thanks to the shortened transport lines and the absence of circular movement within the enterprise.

The layout of shops and machines will

Much the same thing can be said for plans for areas of industrial activities. The attempt to shove all the buildings of an enterprise into one heap is in no way justified and it impairs not only the proper planning of a settlement but also the rational organization of the production. As an illustration, above is the plan accepted for the Nizhegorod auto plant now being built (see Fig. 15).[33]

As is evident from the diagram, the movement of production is particularly complicated. The mechanics' shops are squeezed in between the pressing, forging, rolling, and open-hearth sections which will have an adverse effect on both personnel and machinery. The flow of production not

16. ASSEMBLY-LINE PLAN FOR THE NIZHNINOVGOROD AUTO PLANT.

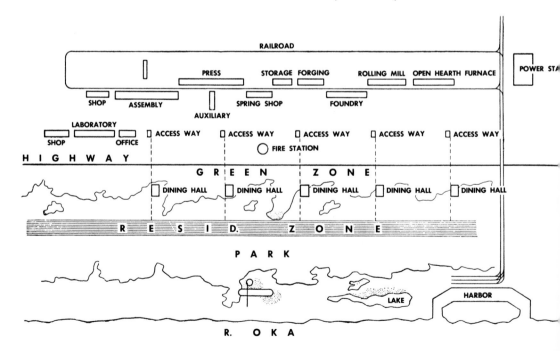

give the enterprise unlimited freedom of movement, will help the enterprise to organize the productive processes themselves in the most rational assembly-line fashion, and will bring the work force closer; and this will have a beneficial effect on productivity and will free it from the necessity of constructing a variety of subsidiary buildings such as branch fire stations, nurseries, dining halls, medical offices, etc.

The placement of factory departments, shops, warehouses, etc. between two lines of transportation (railway and highway) provides an exceptional opportunity to eliminate that chaos and crowding which characterize our plants at present.

The illumination and ventilation of shops under this system will be facilitated since in front of their transparent facades will be nothing but greenery or arteries of transport—not other shops. This will also increase the workers' production significantly. **In general, without spending an extra kopeck but frequently even saving one, we can better organize the productive process and make the work healthier and extend the working hours of men and machines by rational arrangement of the buildings** (and also of the machines in them).

Finally, in order not to have to return again to layout of productive systems, we should say a word here about the type of buildings for them.

Here (and frequently in the West as well) the fact that **contemporary production is based on a process flow** (conveyor) is far from being understood. Meanwhile this intrinsically new principle of organization requires a different layout of the ma-

chines and, therefore, of the buildings than we had until now. The conveyor, like all other transportation, must have a linear course, intersected only at those points of contact with processed material (assemblage), but not in the processing of the material itself. The principle is not altered even when circular conveyors are used (in bakeries, for example), where the flow is not intersected.

This situation, as well as the **ever-increasing significance of machines** due to the introduction of new processes with huge capacities, means that questions of the construction of factory buildings must be seen in an entirely new light.

We have a long-standing attitude about the expediency of multistory and wide buildings. Our opinion grows out of the fact that the layout of land plots in the West is connected with planning on the line system but that the expense of the land necessitates the upward growth of the complex. In taking over mechanically this experience from the West we do not make the necessary modifications for our own circumstances. We have said enough concerning the advantage of the linear plan; with us, where the price of the land is practically nil, it is a complete waste to spend money on vertical substantial buildings which will long outlast the machines they house. **If we would accept narrow, one-story industrial buildings, we could save considerably on their expense.** Thus in these buildings **foundations become unnecessary** since the **floor** (for instance, made of xylolite[35]) **will lie directly on the ground as will the machines. The walls could be made of glass in wood or metal frames** resting on a light

foundation (for example, one-cinder-block thick on the north, one-half on the south).

Supports (columns, pillars, walls, etc.) **could be made of ordinary wood, and, where necessary, of reinforced concrete or metal constructions; overhead girders can be light beams** except where this would be dangerous or in "hot" departments. **The roofs** could best be **covered with tar paper,** a cheap and lightweight material, extremely easy to produce.[36]

It is evident that **this kind of construction** would last from 20 to 30 years, i.e., about the same length of time as the machines, and would cost about **3–4 times less** than brick buildings [i.e., $\frac{1}{3} - \frac{1}{4}$ as much].

Therefore, **in any planning of new buildings and factories and in the replanning of those already existing, it is necessary wherever possible to avoid the parallel distribution of units** (and machines), **to avoid multilevel buildings and deviations from straight lines, never fearing large expanses of territory for industrial activities** nor the construction of additional connecting offices.

It is self-evident that in any planning for the layout of such plants, at the basis must be the most rational and economical organization of the technological processes of the given production. Moreover, the planner must constantly keep in mind the creation of healthy and safe conditions for man, for which, above all, are necessary light and air.

6 THE NEW ORGANIZATION OF LIFE [36a]

In order to establish basic principles for the construction of the residential sectors of Soviet settlements during our transitional period, we must first enunciate clearly those problems which will present themselves in the immediate years ahead, since even the simplest constructional investments must be relied upon for over a period of from 25 to 40 years. In the course of this time, every change in our way of life will be closely reflected in our residential construction which depends on the stage of our development at the time of construction. Thus **in building a separate kitchen for every 2 or 3 rooms, we are wasting ten times the amount of funds and energy that would be necessary for the construc-**

tion of one large factory kitchen or food-combine with a chain of communal dining halls or of subsidiary kitchens near the general housing area. Today this question is settled by attempts to build both the separate and the collective, but since we have very little money at present, we end up building primarily the individual kitchens and not large-scale mechanized ones.

Exactly the same is true of nurseries and kindergartens for our children. While building separate apartments for each worker, we would like at the same time, to create a chain of nurseries and kindergartens for their children, but, since we do not have the means at present to build either of these, we must decide in favor of individual family apartments and not general institutions for the bringing up of children.

The question must be decided one way or the other.

If we attempt to do both, it would mean an increase of $1\frac{1}{2}$ times over the present outlay for the construction of living space, which, given the present housing crisis, is hardly feasible for us without lowering the quota of living area available per person.

And, therefore, the first question we must decide is the matter of priority, or more accurately, which matter should receive more attention: should it be on the

collectivization of the most significant needs of the populace or on the improvement of individual services?

It seems to us that there can be only one answer: prime attention must be on the creation of institutions for collective services for social needs.

We are brought to this conclusion not simply by considerations of a programmatic and theoretical nature. **The problem of workers' teams** has already, today, become a very real question in the long-range development of our economy. In the current fiscal year our very first industries are going into operation, and already the supply-market of workers has diminished considerably. **Tomorrow, when our new gigantic industries demand hundreds of thousands and millions of workers, the rural countryside will not be able to provide these millions** since the development of agriculture, the exploitation of huge unsettled areas, the development of new branches and processes, will also demand new working hands. **We will find these hands by freeing woman from housework, and this is possible only through collectivizing our way of life.**

Besides, the extreme crisis in housing and **the problem** posed by Marx and Lenin **regarding a new method of distribution of population raises the question of control-**

ling the migration to our present cities. An alternative would be to use for production the already existing able-bodied labor reserves of the female portion of the population of cities.

Statistical analysis of the composition of workers' families tells us that collectivization of the living services of the population would produce about a 30% increase in workers from the same number of adults in the city population, of which 40–50% would be occupied in providing these services, while 50–60% would be freed for production. In other words, 15–18% of the overall city population can go into augmenting the productive labor force, which would mean an increase of $1\frac{1}{2}$ times the number of workers, with no increase in the city population.

Research carried out for the programming of the construction of Stalingrad fully bore out these conclusions.

The second major contemporary problem—the raising of the productive capacity of labor—will find its best answer in the collectivization of the life services since this will eliminate worry about the obtaining of products, fuel, etc.

Finally, **the problem of raising the standard of living of the population also finds its solution in the collectivization of the life services,** even with our contemporary productive capacity of the labor force. Freeing woman from the household and making her into a worker will increase the family's earnings; only from 40 to 50% of these additional earnings need go toward the expenses of the family while 50–60% will be used to raise the standard of living.

Therefore, collectivization of the life

services of the population provides:

1) **the freedom of woman from domestic slavery;**

2) **a reduction, and in places elimination, of the demands for a flow of new workers into the city;**

3) **a reduction of demand for new residential construction;**

4) **an increase in the productive capacity of the labor force;**

5) **an increase in the standard of living of the working population; and**

6) **an advance to a higher cultural level for mankind.**

In posing the problem so, does this mean that collective feeding and education will have to take children away from their parents?

Not in the least.

The matter of the healthy influence of children on adults—parental instincts, etc. —can in no way be ignored.

Right now we are only concerned with the premise of introducing social education for youngsters. Moreover, in every case **the closest bond between the parents and the children must be guaranteed.** Parents, unless they have been deprived of the rights of parenthood by committing a crime, must have the privilege of coming to take the child at any time.

Only through extensive educational processes can the influence of the individual family be replaced by the influence of the collective. This matter can by no means be solved mechanically.

Our problem today is one of creating the material foundation for collective education of children. There can be no question of compulsion as of now.

In building special institutions for the life and education of children (closely connected with the adults' home) we are establishing **only the necessary conditions so that parents, when they wish, may send their children to these institutions.**

Meanwhile, by depriving families of certain individual services and not allowing them to arrange this and that as they please, we of course do to some extent influence the population toward the organization of collective education. This will not, however, mean compulsion and even less so the worsening of already existing conditions, since **family apartments in the already existing cities are more than sufficient in number for the entire transitional period, while new construction will provide more, not less, living space for the family.** Thus, it is not so much a matter of forbidding parents to keep their children as it is the creation of new living space for children by building specially equipped children's institutions near the buildings for general dwelling. This will be done by economizing on the construction of other building (i.e., elimination of individual kitchens, entranceways, corridors, pantries, etc.).

So far as collective feeding is concerned, we must go about this by creating healthful means for the gradual elimination of individual preparation of food by establishing collective dining rooms. Also, in the transitional period we must provide for the construction of subsidiary kitchens in the dwellings, which—until the later period of food-combines (which produce semiprocessed staples)—will play an important role in organizing inexpensive feeding of the population and result in a significant saving

17. FIVE-YEAR-PLAN CONSTRUCTION OF THE INDUSTRY OF COLLECTIVIZED VICTUALING.

ACCORDING TO NARPIT

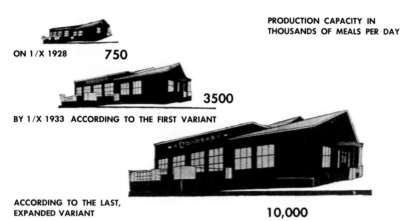

PRODUCTION CAPACITY IN
THOUSANDS OF MEALS PER DAY

ON 1/X 1928   **750**

3500

BY 1/X 1933 ACCORDING TO THE FIRST VARIANT

ACCORDING TO THE LAST,
EXPANDED VARIANT

10,000

of time. These subsidiary kitchens are to be arranged one for every 25–50 rooms; that is, about one for every 10–20 families. They should be designed in such a way that they can be changed over into conventional living space once the need for them has passed.

Much the same can be said for laundries. The creation of good and inexpensive mechanical laundries (placed to best advantage in connection with the public baths) will completely free women from this barbaric task. But we should also provide for small mechanical installations where male and female workers can, with a minimum of effort, wash their underthings. The installation of these laundries will also call for a minimal expenditure, and it will be a great advantage for the lower-paid group of the population.

Thus we see that **institutions for collective feeding of the population, collective education of children, as well as mechanized laundries—these are the first necessary elements of collective life that must be provided for in new construction.**

The usual (alas, not original!) argument that is leveled against this is that the system will destroy the traditional family order, that it will entail loosening up and eventual complete disintegration of the family.

It is not difficult to see that this argument is nothing more than a recrudescence of bourgeois ideology; indeed
with the image of the life of the people, with their collective relationships, with their collective mode of living, their imaginations, their outlooks, their understanding, in a word, their consciousness also

changes. What is it that substantiates the history of ideas, if not the fact that the mental activity transforms itself together with the material activity? The leading ideas of any given time have always been the ideas of the ruling class. (K. Marx) [39]

Yes, the traditional way of life will change in proportion to the degree of collectivization. But we are not at all against changes nor the elimination of the family mode of life, one of the survivals of a form of slavery—that of woman in the bourgeois world.

Abolition of the family! Even extreme radicals throw up their hands in horror when they speak of this shameful communist proposal.

On what is today's bourgeois family based? On capital, on private gain. In its fully developed form, it exists only for the bourgeoisie, but has its corollaries: the forced family-less state of the proletarians and public prostitution.

The bourgeois family will inevitably collapse together with the collapse of these corollaries, and together the two will vanish with the vanishing of capital.

Do you reproach us for wanting to stop the exploitation of children by their parents? We plead guilty to the charge!

Our determination to replace domestic education by social, implies (you declare) a disregard for the most sacred of relationships.

But the education you provide, is it not socially determined? Is it not determined by the social conditions within whose framework you educate? Is it not determined directly or indirectly by soci-

ety, acting through the schools, etc.? The influence of society upon education was not a discovery of the communists! They merely propose to change the character of the process, by withdrawing education from the influence of the ruling class.

Bourgeois phrasemaking about the family and education, about the intimate relationships between parents and children, becomes more and more nauseating in proportion as the development of large-scale industry severs all the family ties of the proletarians, and in proportion as proletarian children are transformed into mere articles of commerce and instruments of labor.

—But you communists want to make women common property!—shrieks the bourgeois chorus.

The bourgeois regards his wife as nothing but an instrument of production. He is told that the means of production are to be utilized in common. How can he help thinking that this implies the communization of women as well as other things?

He never dreams for a moment that our main purpose is to insure that women shall no longer occupy the position of a mere instrument of production.

Besides, nothing could be more absurd than the virtuous indignation of our bourgeois as regards the official communization of women which the communists are supposed to advocate. Communists do not need to introduce community of women; it has almost invariably existed.

The members of the bourgeoisie, not content with having the wives and daughters of proletarians at their disposal

18. CONSTRUCTION OF FACTORY KITCHENS.

ACCORDING TO NARPIT

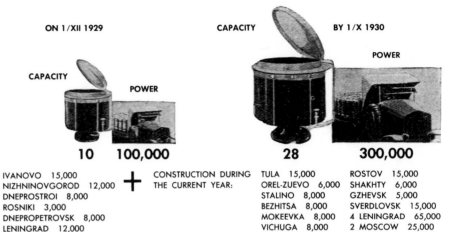

ON 1/XII 1929

CAPACITY

POWER

10   100,000

CAPACITY   BY 1/X 1930

POWER

28   300,000

IVANOVO	15,000		
NIZHNINOVGOROD	12,000		
DNEPROSTROI	8,000		
ROSNIKI	3,000		
DNEPROPETROVSK	8,000		
LENINGRAD	12,000		
4 MOSCOW	42,000		

+ CONSTRUCTION DURING THE CURRENT YEAR:

TULA	15,000	ROSTOV	15,000
OREL-ZUEVO	6,000	SHAKHTY	6,000
STALINO	8,000	GZHEVSK	5,000
BEZHITSA	8,000	SVERDLOVSK	15,000
MOKEEVKA	8,000	4 LENINGRAD	65,000
VICHUGA	8,000	2 MOSCOW	25,000
SHUIA	8,000	BAKU	8,000

(to say nothing of public prostitution) find one of their chief pleasures in seducing one another's wives!

Bourgeois marriage is, in actual fact, the community of wives. At worst, communists can only be charged with wanting to replace a hypocritical and concealed community of women by an official and frankly acknowledged community. Moreover, it is self-evident that the abolition of the present system of production will lead to the disappearance of that form of the community of women which results therefrom—to the disappearance of official and unofficial prostitution. (K. Marx—F. Engels, Communist Manifesto).

It is hard to think of a better answer to the clamorers against the new way of life, and against the establishment of a material

basis for the breakup of the family. One cannot but regret that in certain circles of our party, the bourgeois ideology is so strong, that, with a diligence worthy of a less petty purpose, they think up ever new arguments for retaining the double bed as a permanent and compulsory item in the worker's home!

It is easy to see that the resistance of these circles to the growing movement of the new masses of workers toward a new way of life "reflects the typical resistance of obsolete classes" (J. Stalin, speech at the XVI Party Congress).

Along with institutions for collectivized education of children and institutions for collectivized feeding, the problem of creating a network of repair shops must be met as well as the establishing of cultural and educational works (libraries, clubs, etc.).

The programs for these institutions must be carefully thought out in advance.

It is best, therefore, to organize a **network of repair shops at any given stage along cooperative lines** (for example, artels of the handicapped). In organizing libraries, the American system should be taken into account and adapted to our needs (see Kravchenko's book, *Toward a Single Main Library System*, published by Glz, 1929, price: 10 kopecks). Smaller libraries for more current literature should be established in our communal dwelling units (for example, in the dining rooms). These should be connected with district libraries and those, in turn, with regional libraries and so on—up to the central, all-union library. Every citizen should have the possibility of requesting for himself any book in the country. **This system** would cut down tremendously **on the** number of books

which have to be printed and at the same time would allow anyone who wished to receive any book. It would be possible to charge for this either by subscription or by single payment, as desired. **No special reading rooms would have to be built** (except in district libraries or in libraries affiliated with scientific institutions), since anyone can improve himself by reading and working with a book at home and in the summer by reading it out in the garden or on the terrace, etc.

Reading rooms in small libraries and in **many institutions connected with individual and isolated entertainment and learning will disappear because of their uselessness** (for example, those in maternity homes, dairies, kitchens, children's administrations, in many educational units, factory-workshop schools, in a number of buildings for the departments of economics and medi-

cine, in technological institutions, school laboratories, etc.).

Similarly, the construction of **special accommodations for physical culture is completely superfluous.** It must be clear to everyone how absurd it would be to drive this work indoors in summer; and winter sports and physical culture must be so planned that they are connected with ice (mountains, ice-skates, etc.) and snow (skis). It is time for us to begin to become accustomed to fresh air and the cold. Youth must first be toughened up; let the parades come later. It seems to me that our physical culture experts will solve this problem brilliantly. This does not, of course, preclude the installation of some apparatus in social accommodations (for example in clubs) without, however, the creation of special rooms for them, etc.

A couple of words about the organization of the life of children of school age. Here we must examine the question of dormitories for school children and school camps. All that we have said prior to this [pp. 74, 75 ff.] about the construction of living areas for children of pre-school age is also relevant to those of school age, with the only distinction being that the latter can live at a somewhat greater distance from the adults. Besides this, the methods of an education directed toward a closer link between it and production must be carefully worked out.

Thus, the gradual collectivization of social services, the interrelating of schools with production, and the new organization of physical culture will provide us a basic economy in our new buildings.

19. SCOPE OF COLLECTIVIZED FEEDING OF MAJOR INDUSTRIAL GROUPS UNDER THE FIVE-YEAR-PLAN.

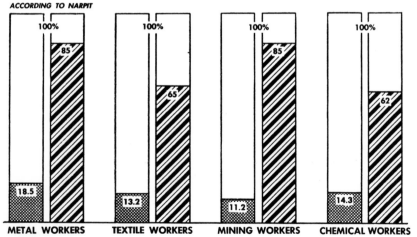

ACCORDING TO NARPIT

METAL WORKERS · TEXTILE WORKERS · MINING WORKERS · CHEMICAL WORKERS

 ON 1/X 1929
BY 1/X 1933

As a result, **we must have the following buildings in the residential area:**

1) **dwelling houses;**

2) **dining rooms with small related facilities for collective relaxation** (libraries, billiards, chess);

3) **institutions for pre-school children** (nurseries and kindergartens);

4) **dormitories for school-age children;**

5) **district and local clubs** (culture palaces and rest homes) with local (district) libraries, sporting fields, etc.

In addition, it would not be a bad idea to have in parks several café-pavilions, areas for games and physical culture (tennis, volleyball), and also, where possible, **piers for sailing, rowing, and motor boats.** This would cost us only kopecks, but would be extremely useful.

●

General conclusion: **the residential zone must be planned and built as a unified economic arrangement of a socialistic type in which will be provided all the necessary conditions for the collectivization of communal, social, and cultural needs of the population** (feeding, education of children and young people, medical care, baths, laundries, repair shops, water supplies, sewers, transportation, clubs, etc.).

The system of cooperation and collectivization of all the most important parts of the social way of life and cultural services must, in the last analysis, make possible the use of all the labor resources of the population. In particular, to use the labor of women freed from the demands of home economy, the labor of the handi- capped,[40] **and also the organized use of the labor of children and adolescents by a system of education that is based upon industrial and agricultural production.**

In organizing life in buildings and settlements constructed in the new way, any elements that might coerce people into the new way of life must be totally excluded. The new way of life must be born as a natural result of the new organization of labor and housing and of the proper organization of institutions for collectivized social services to meet the needs of the population.

●

7

THE LOCATION OF BUILDINGS

The placement of the separate buildings in the living zone is also of significance. To begin with, the illumination of the interior of edifices by sunlight is mandatory, especially in view of the criminal practice—not only in the big capitalist countries but also here among ourselves—of placing buildings in such a way that there are many areas, including living spaces, which get no direct sunlight at all.

Nonetheless, it must be said that there are many projects (Stalingrad, for example) where our planners deprive whole sectors of sunlight and, at the same time, have the effrontery to call them "socialistic." Needless to say, it is a fine kind of socialism that deprives a worker of the sunlight!

Therefore, it is **essential** to demand that **all dwelling houses, if there are two rows of apartments, be placed along the meridian (from south to north), but if** there be only one, it should then face south or south-east.** The disposition of living dwellings helter-skelter must not be allowed unless the "offshoot" (i.e., running east to west) has one row of dwellings facing the south and in addition the "offshoot" does not shade the dwellings situated behind it.

Besides this, **no construction should be permitted** (including baths, corridors, toilets, etc.) **which does not get some sun every day.**

We must also **categorically eliminate the disgraceful congestion in the layout of buildings that is the rule in cities.** In general, it would be more correct to lay out buildings in one line, leaving in front of their windows forest, field, or water. If conditions are such that traffic requires that the transparent facades of parallel rows of buildings face each other, then a wide free space should be left between them of no less than 75–100 m (depending on the size and height of the building).

The usual argument against such placement is that it would complicate and make more expensive the social services in the community. It must be said, however, that this is far from being so. **By laying out the buildings in one line we will not lengthen the pavements, water pipes, sewers, and electric lines but will actually shorten them.** This is due to the fact that we will then have a single unbent line which will make unnecessary the innumerable offshoots common at present.

In parallel rows of buildings, we can run the sewer, water, and electric lines along and under the houses rather than through the streets as now, intersecting the houses roughly in the middle of their sides.

Finally, **it will be necessary to end the practice of combining in the same building so many diverse installations for different services.** For example, the inclusion of stores in dwelling houses infests them with rodents, etc.; it sharply increases the cost of the store and hastens eventual deterioration of the building; placing nurseries and kindergartens in dwellings breeds epidemics among children; the building of cinemas will dirty the residences and expose them to fire, etc., etc.

The most that should be accommodated directly in dwellings are libraries and study units, and these should be only for the use of the residents.

It goes without saying that the installation in living quarters of productive activity of any kind, except perhaps the very lightest (for example, laundries), should not be allowed under any circumstances.

●

8 THE LIVING CELL

The creation of collectivized dining halls, nurseries, kindergartens, dormitories, laundries, and repair shops **will really break radically with the existing family attitude toward property,** and this will provide the economic premises for the extinction of the family as an economic unit.

This fact allows us to see the residential cells in new buildings as being compartments for separate people united in the collective in which the family, if it exists, does not do so as an economic unit but as a free group of people—united by personality, by kinship, or the like. **The intimate relationships of people will become their own private affair independent of any direct property considerations.** Part of the ex-

penses of the education of children, until fully assumed by society, will be borne by the parents according to their incomes.

We can, therefore, state that these **living cells must be** apportioned **one per person** for the adult population with the option that they may be united in various combinations, have direct connection with each other, and so forth; this will allow the population to live in whatever combination it desires including families, using its living space according to its own tastes and habits.

It therefore **follows** that in constructing new buildings **all living cells must be furnished with the minimum necessary equipment** that is indispensable for man's living quarters. One must move toward a situation in which it would be possible, gradually, to end man's present enslavement by his possessions. Besides, this is consistent with purely economic considerations. The construction of homes along with their equipment of the most essential furniture will make it possible to combine mass production with inexpensive and good furniture.

In order to decide what an individual living cell must look like, what furnishings it must have, its dimensions and internal design, it is necessary that we first of all determine its function (i.e., its significance).

We can **under no circumstances** agree with those comrades who attempt **to**

THE COMMUNIST REVOLUTION IS THE MOST RADICAL RUPTURE WITH EXISTING PROPERTY RELATIONS; NO WONDER THAT ITS DEVELOPMENT INVOLVES THE MOST RADICAL RUPTURE WITH TRADITIONAL IDEAS.   K. MARX – F. ENGELS, *COMMUNIST MANIFESTO*

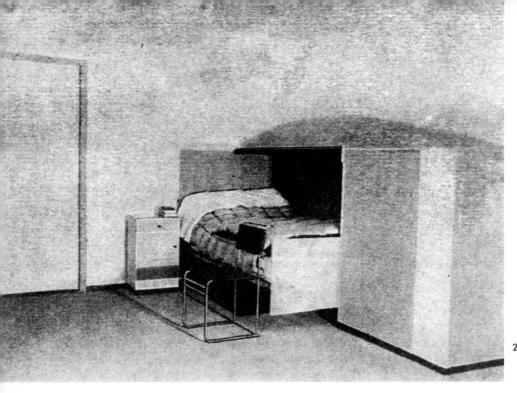

20. BAUHAUS AT DESSAU. **DWELLING ROOM.**[41a]

The individual residential cell (that is, for each person) must provide:

1) for sleeping;

2) for book use, etc.;

3) for individual relaxation;

4) for the safekeeping of one's things that are in constant use (linens, clothing, one's individual everyday items, etc.);

5) for attention to elementary personal hygiene.

Assuming these functions, the individual living cell should have the following minimum equipment:

1) a place to sleep, in form of either a convertible bed or a divan which can turn into a bed at night—or just an ordinary bed;

2) a working table with drawers for objects for intellectual work (notebooks, books, paper, etc.);

3) two or three chairs or an arm chair;

4) a small table;

5) storage for clothes and linens (for example, built into the wall);

6) a wash basin;

7) a medicine cabinet with hygienic supplies and a mirror.

Besides this there should be a shower stall (even if only one for every two rooms).

So equipped, the living cell will transform itself (convert itself): during the day as a work study and quarters for individual relaxation, and at night as a sleeping room.

If these are the purposes of the residential cell, it should have the following minimum dimensions, including the equipment:

a) along the facade (outside wall) 2.8 m,

b) in depth 3 m.

assign the sole role of sleeping cabin to the living cell, and who relegate all the other functions to collectivized buildings.[41] Thus, for example, they think to create a row of studies in each general dwelling for the study of books; for conversation with one's comrades they want special collective sitting rooms; for rest during the day, corresponding resting rooms; etc.

This kind of parceling out of the functions of living is no more than a peculiar exaggeration at the basis of which lies the idea of the lordly suite, applied no longer to the family but to the collective. Actually, what we have here is only a formally modified pattern of the petit-bourgeois dwelling. As a curiosity, one can cite the example of a number of projects for a living cabin in the settlement of the Nizhegorod auto plant where the designers of this sleeping cabin idea have exchanged the "necessity" that finds itself under most middle class beds for a bowl alongside of it! **Transformation of the dwelling unit into a mere toilet is the ideal of the middle-class architect!**

This mistaken conception leads to the situation whereby, giving too much space to collectivized studies, dining rooms, and so on, the authors of the "sleeping cabin" project were forced to cut down so far on the space for the cabins that they will be of less than average comfort.

We must focus attention on these mistakes because **such distortion and errors can discredit the whole idea of the new dwelling.**

This makes 8.4 m². If we take the minimum height as 2.6 m, **then the minimum volume of the living cell will be 21.84 m³.**

It is evident that these measurements are minimal and, with the slightest opportunity, should be increased.

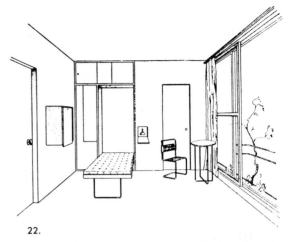

22.

As an illustration we give below two variants of such compartments worked out by ourselves. The drawing in Fig. 21 shows cells having the minimum dimensions 8.4 m² or 21.84 m³. Figures 22–23 illustrate the general appearance of such a cell with a bed that folds into the wall.

21. MINIMAL DWELLING UNIT (8.4 m²)
WITH SLIDING WINDOWS   WITH SLIDING TRANSPARENT WALLS

23.

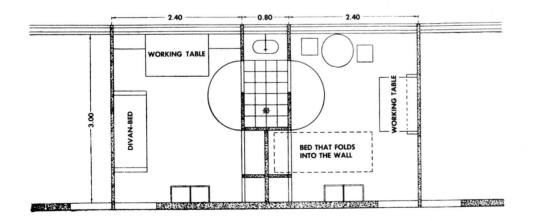

2.40   0.80   2.40

WORKING TABLE

DIVAN-BED

3.00

WORKING TABLE

BED THAT FOLDS
INTO THE WALL

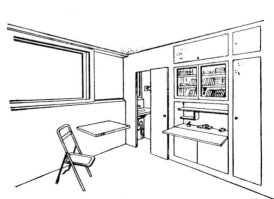

24. PLAN OF GROUND FLOOR.

PLAN OF SECOND FLOOR. 25.

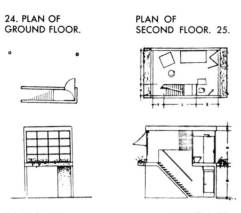

30. AXONOMETRIC VIEW.

26. FACADE.   **SECTION. 27.**

Figures 24–30 show the plan, section, elevation, and the internal and general appearance of the living cell worked out by Stroikom RSFSR.[42] This compartment has a floor area of 14 m² and a volume of 39.2 m³, has a special cabinet for shower and toilet, and has two transparent walls.

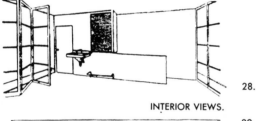

28.

INTERIOR VIEWS.

29.

The examples of plans of living cells here may be recommended as an initial step for the further work of planners for whom it is **important** that the basic premise be understood **that man in any case will be spending about half his life in this space.** For this reason, reducing it to "little cabins" or worse still into "closets" makes a mockery of the concept of man's new dwelling.

From this arises the necessity for special attention to the question of aesthetics and hygiene in the equipping and painting of the living cells. **All the attainments of contemporary architecture** and applied art must be **mobilized so that a healthy and happy life for man can be achieved** in the minimum which the living cell offers.

Unobstructed ventilation must be unconditionally guaranteed, for which, incidentally, it is not in the least necessary to construct ventilating ducts, which are still expensive; we need only install air vents— or even better, moving windows (on rollers) (see Fig. 23) or even whole sliding walls (see Fig. 22).

If means are insufficient to provide 8.4 square meters per person, then showers could be planned for 12 to 15 people.

Every kind of cornice, fretwork, open shelf, etc. must be avoided as a source of dust and infection (contamination). Partitions and exterior property walls must be avoided since it would be thoughtless to keep light out of the interior.

The same holds true for the various rags with which our inhabitants do so love to "prettify" their dwelling, turning it into such a dusty accumulation of useless trash.

The challenge to the contemporary architect is how to arrange for more light, air, happiness, and simplicity.

9 COLLECTIVIZED INSTITUTIONS FOR THE NEEDS OF THE POPULATION

Institutions for children should be divided into the following groups:

1) nurseries for children up to 3 years of age;

2) kindergartens for those from 4 to 7;

3) dormitories and camps for those from 8 to 14;

4) dormitories and camps for those from 15 to 18.

Nurseries can be organized in two ways: 1) for 45 to 60 children; 2) for 90 to 120 children. The smaller number of children in the nursery is determined by the calculation of services rendered the separate age levels; the larger limit is determined by the level beyond which the accumulation of children of the same age represents too great a danger of infectious disease. **In my opinion the most reasonable total would be from 45 to 60 children for nurseries.**

The arrangement of the nursery depends on its size. According to the specifications of Narkomzdrav the greatest volume of space necessary per child in the nursery is from 50 to 55 m^3 including the service and related accommodations.[43]

Kindergartens, according to the specifications of Narkompros,[44] consist of groups of 20 children each. It is not possible to concentrate in one accommodation more than three groups, i.e., 60 children. The largest volume of space necessary for children is determined by Narkompros to be from 50 to 60 m^3 per child.

School dormitories (for children from 8 to 14 years of age) are recommended by Narkompros to be arranged for from 80 to 100 children. Each child should have from 50 to 60 m^3 of space.

Youth dormitories (for ages 15 to 18) need not be built at all since the adolescents can live in the general residences together with adults or in special collective dwellings differentiated from the others only by the absence of nurseries and kindergartens.

The ceiling height for all these accommodations is calculated to be roughly 4 m and could be reduced without harm to 3.2 m as long as the volume is maintained at 50 m^3 for each child and adolescent, regardless of age.

Not included in this cubic measurement

WE WILL CREATE EXEMPLARY INSTITUTIONS, DINING HALLS, NURSERIES, WHICH WILL FREE WOMAN FROM HOME CARES.
. . . THESE INSTITUTIONS, LIBERATING WOMAN FROM THE POSITION OF A DOMESTIC SLAVE, SPRING UP EVERYWHERE WHERE THERE IS THE SLIGHTEST POSSIBILITY FOR THEM TO DO SO.
LENIN

are: 1) kitchens, since food will be prepared either in factory kitchens or (under the system of food-combines) in the kitchen–dining room of the dormitory; 2) special school accommodations (laboratories, auxiliary rooms, etc.), since these must be quartered in special buildings and counted as services for the dormitories.

The number of children per thousand people is approximately as follows:

    1) under 3 years..................100
    2) from 4 to 7 60
    3) from 8 to 14 140

Altogether, of those under 14 there are 300 and from 15 to 17 (inclusive) there are 65.

It must be kept in mind that these figures vary for different categories of the population and for various cities. Thus, the number of children per thousand of population under 14 in Moscow is 236, in Sverdlovsk—279, in Ivanovo-Voznesensk—283, in Motovilikh—349, at the Votkinskii Plant—342, etc.

In the layout of children's quarters, the following must be taken into account:

1) the lower the age of the children, the closer they should be to their parents and the easier it should be for them to communicate with each other;

2) the older the children, the closer they should be to collectivized and productive institutions and activities in order that the influence of their parents gradually be replaced by that of the collective;

3) between children close in age there must be provided a constant communication and proximity for their mutual influence; this is important for their development.

It will, therefore, be correct, if in plan-ning dormitories, we will lay out the nurseries and kindergartens of the residences with covered walkways (but not with interior corridors, in order to avoid spreading of contagious diseases).

It would be best that the accommodations for children of school age be situated in special residences, connected with the school buildings.

Buildings for children of pre-school age should never be multistoried.[45] The best would be a one-story building having a sliding glass south wall with a small low open terrace in front of it containing a shallow pool for running water. Everything must, of course, be surrounded by greenery. The distance from the children's residence (nurseries as well as kindergartens) to the residence for grownups should be from 20 to 30 meters. The children's residence should be on the side of the adult quarters that is away from the productive zone.

●

The following figures should determine the dimensions of the general dwelling.

Assuming that each dwelling should have a nursery and kindergarten, we see that:

1) the smallest general dwelling may be organized for 400 people (i.e., about 100–125 families), 300 adults and 100 children of pre-school age;

2) the largest general dwelling will be for 800 people (i.e., 200–250 families), 600 adults and 200 children of pre-school age.[46]

It is self-evident that these figures must be considered as average and therefore deviations from them are inevitable in individual cases. These variations can be compensated for by relocating orphans in the children's residences, and single people and adolescents in the adult quarters.

The so-called communal body which includes dining room (with kitchen), barber shop, small library, and recreation rooms (billiards, chess, etc.) would best be put into a separate building connected with the adult residence by a heated corridor.[47] The space necessary for this would be on the order of 1 m^3 per person. If the quarters for recreation and the small library were put together, the average height of the communal body would then be about 4.5–5 m, whence the general cubic capacity of these buildings would be set at from 5 to 6 m^3 per person.

By calculating several shifts for the operation of the dining room, its area—and consequently the volume of the communal body—can be reduced by 30–50%.

●

31.
EXTERNAL VIEW.

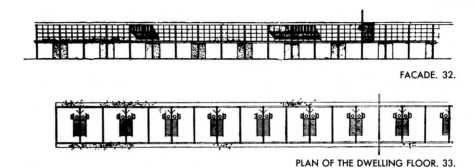

FACADE. 32.

PLAN OF THE DWELLING FLOOR. 33.

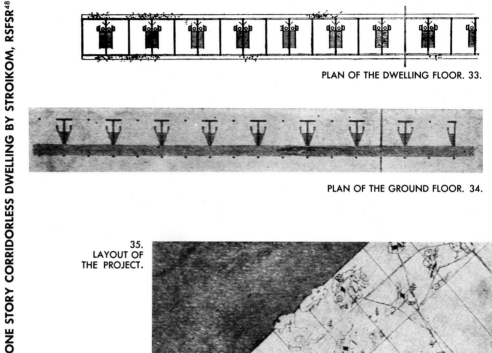

PLAN OF THE GROUND FLOOR. 34.

ONE STORY CORRIDORLESS DWELLING BY STROIKOM, RSFSR[48]

10 BLOCKING OUT THE LIVING CELLS AND INSTITUTIONS

The amalgamation of residential cells, nurseries, kindergartens, and of the communal body into blocks can take the widest variety of forms.

Whatever the decision may be, however, one must keep in mind the correlation between child and adult population figures, which determines the maximum and minimum dimensions of the blocks. It is self-evident that, on the one hand, a number of these blocks may be joined together into one general block (which is not particularly expedient) or, on the other hand, can be split up. (For example, for a single nursery and one kindergarten there can be 2, 3, 4, etc. adult dwelling buildings.) As regards communal bodies, if a mechanized kitchen and food-combine are present then it is best to build them for no more than 300—400 diners.

Taking into consideration previous

35.
LAYOUT OF
THE PROJECT.

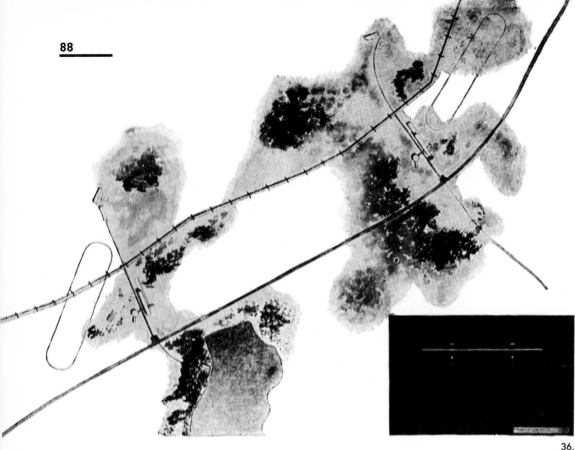

36.

LAYOUT OF THE PLAN[50]

37.

ONE STORY CORRIDORLESS DWELLING BY STROIKOM, RSFSR[49]

construction experience up to this point, one can recommend the following schemes for architectural organization of blocks:

1. A one-story corridorless block (proposed by Stroikom RSFSR, Figs. 24–55) in which the residential units are arranged in one uninterrupted ribbon, and, moreover, each unit has a separate entrance underneath the house—which is up on pilotis. Stations of the transportation routes with attendant communal facilities are placed at certain intervals in front of and parallel to this [continuous] dwelling body. The station is connected with the dwelling body by a covered walkway. An extension of this walkway connects the dwelling body and the station with the children's residence (nurseries and kindergartens are placed in a checkerboard pattern). This arrangement is suitable for agricultural enterprises in the south, although it suffers from severe shortcomings; it requires a very complicated movement system (for every 300 people, one kilometer of road). Thanks to the absence of corridors, this system gives an exceptionally good economic relationship between the square meters of dwelling area and the cubic volume of the building (about 3.2), which makes it possible to expand the living space per person to 14 cubic meters; however, this is exclusive of the building of auxiliary facilities for each group of rooms (auxiliary kitchens, boilers, etc.).

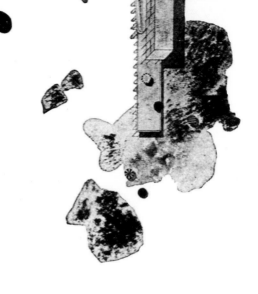

38. AXONOMETRIC VIEW.[51]

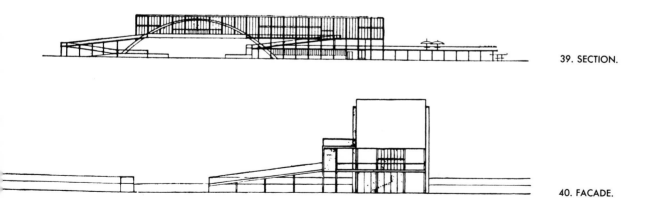

39. SECTION.

40. FACADE.

(COMMUNAL BODY)
STATION

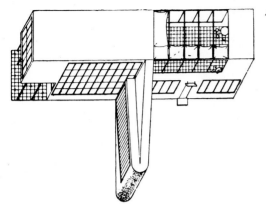

41. AXONOMETRIC VIEW.

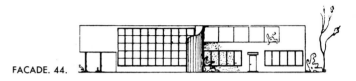

FACADE. 44.

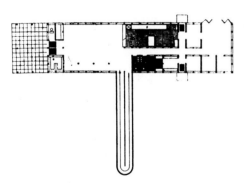

42. PLAN OF GROUND FLOOR.

43. PLAN OF SECOND FLOOR.

45. SECTION.

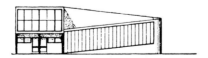

46. FACADE.

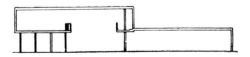

47. SECTION.

CLUB

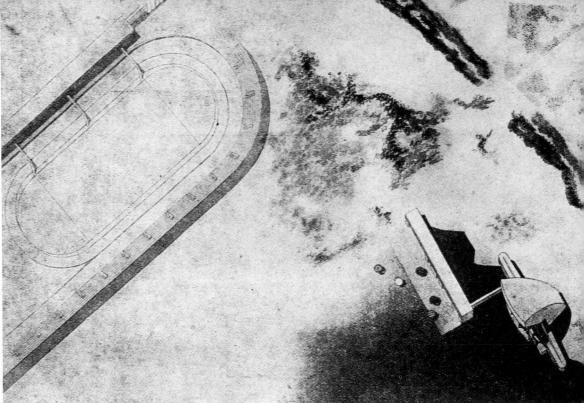

48. AXONOMETRIC VIEW.[52]

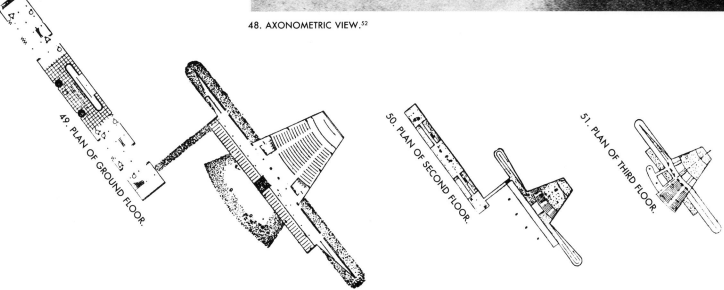

49. PLAN OF GROUND FLOOR.

50. PLAN OF SECOND FLOOR.

51. PLAN OF THIRD FLOOR.

52. REST AND CULTURE PARK.⁵³

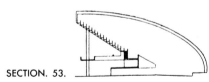

SECTION. 53.

FACADE. 54.

CLUB

FACADE. 55.

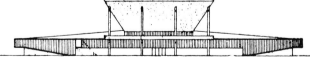

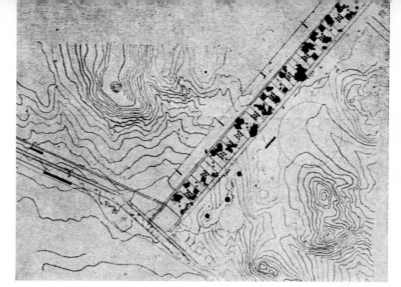

LAYOUT. 56.

OSA SETTLEMENT

2. A system of separate houses for 32 people each with 2 per room (proposed by OSA, see Figs. 56–58).[54] The communal quarters are laid out in a hall with two glass walls, and the arrangement is not linked to the roadways but depends exclusively on local topography. Besides those mentioned in the previous project, a disadvantage is an extremely unsatisfactory relationship of the area to the cubic content of the buildings.

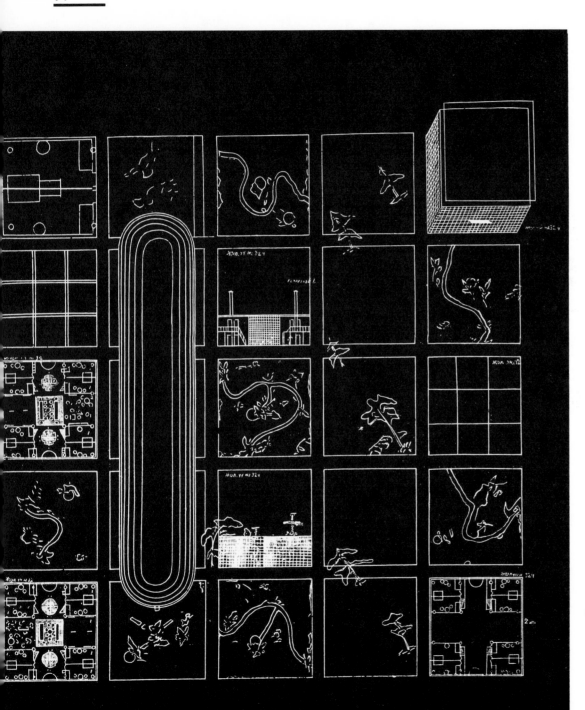

57. **BLOCK**.
(PLAN, AXONOMETRIC VIEW, FACADE, AND SECTION)

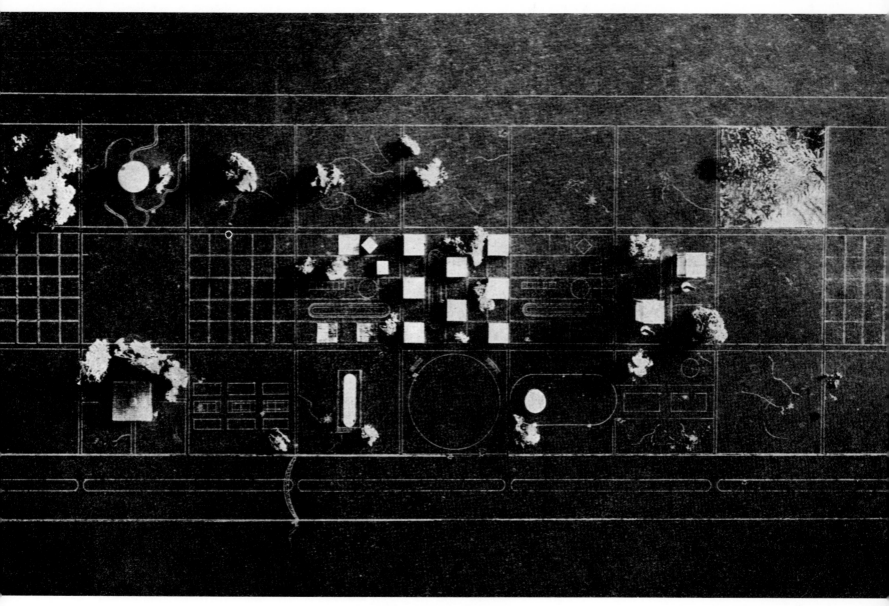

58. **MODEL OF THE OSA SETTLEMENT.**

59.

3. The same solution but with "sky-scrapers" (see Figs. 59–64).[55]

Besides the aforementioned shortcomings, must be added the expensive elevators and the complicated construction of the building.

4. The same solutions but with bigger blocks; in part this will correct the aforementioned defects.

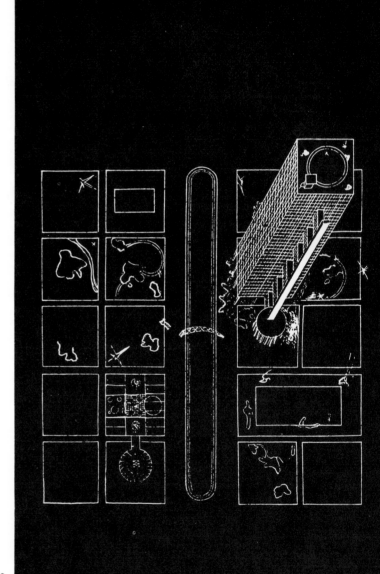

60.

61. GENERAL VIEW OF THE SETTLEMENT. **SKYSCRAPERS**.

OSA

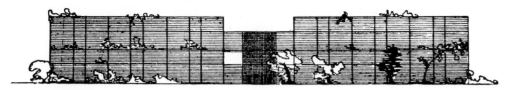

62. FACADE.

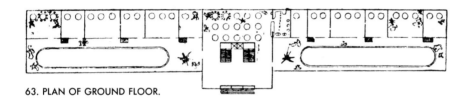

63. PLAN OF GROUND FLOOR.

64. PLAN OF SECOND AND FOURTH FLOORS.

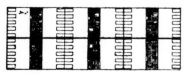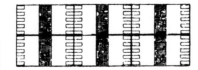

OSA

5. **Finally we come to the projects that we have worked out in two variations for a three-story block for 400–800 people (see Figs. 21–23 and 65–72).**[56]

The first variant gives a three-story block with one corridor, in which the residential unit consists of identical (standardized) groups of 10 residential cells in each [vertical] group, of which two (on the first floor) must accommodate a couple while the other eight (on the second and third floors) are single compartments.

Auxiliary kitchens are installed either on the ground floor or in one of the residential cells (as temporary quarters which can be changed at any time).

Each of these [vertical] groups of rooms is equipped with bath and shower (third floor) and double baths (second floor). All cells can be united, without any changes, into apartments of 2, 3, or 4 rooms.

The second variant of this offers the same residence building but with corridors on each floor and with identical residential units; moreover, services are placed on each floor near the stairway [not illustrated].

Connected with the dwelling unit are the dining room and recreation room (together), the kindergarten or the nursery [see Fig. 70].

The construction of the building is lightened (wooden or reinforced-concrete framework with fibrolite, wood, or organic silicate in-filling) with no partition walls or foundations. The flat roofs are arranged as basins (with no drains).

We try for maximum simplicity and clarity in external appearance and plan.

The only decorations are the window boxes under each window for flowers.

In the residential unit, for one square meter of living area there are 4.5–5 cubic meters of volume. This makes it possible to expand the living area per person to 10.5–12 square meters per 55–60 cubic meters of construction per person, including the communal elements.

Without exception all accommodations including baths, corridors, toilets, stairways, etc.—right up to the very top—are lit by direct sunlight.

With very minor structural changes, such a block can be built from brick or almost any other material.

This solution gives one kilometer of road for 2,000 people and demands 5 times less transportation planning than the first (Stroikom) project.

Two schemes of the layout of such blocks are possible (house-communes):

1) In a line along the highway.

2) End-on to the highway—moreover the buildings are situated in separate parallel blocks for from 300 to 600 adults [see Fig. 70]. Each block should be about 100 meters from the next. This would mean one kilometer for 4,000–8,000 people. In Moscow, in spite of its insane congestion, there are no more people per kilometer of pavement.

All these projects (along with many others) **undoubtedly need further elaboration and, in particular, practical testing.** One thing is certain: **the creative thought of the contemporary architect-engineer must be mobilized to find a better solution to these problems.** It is necessary to solve a number of still unclear questions concerning the greatest economic advantage of each alternative plan under different climatic conditions; it is also necessary to search for the shrewdest solutions to the plan, for new combinations, etc., etc.

AUXILIARY KITCHEN ON THE GROUND FLOOR NEED NOT BE INSTALLED. INSTEAD, A FEW ROOMS ON THE FIRST FLOOR CAN BE SEPARATED OFF FOR AUXILIARY KITCHENS TO BE DISPOSED AS A TEMPORARY MEASURE. AT ANY TIME THESE CAN BE RECONVERTED TO DWELLING ROOMS (SEE FIG. 69). IN WHICH CASE THE GROUND FLOOR IS LEFT FREE (SEE FIGS. 71 AND 72).

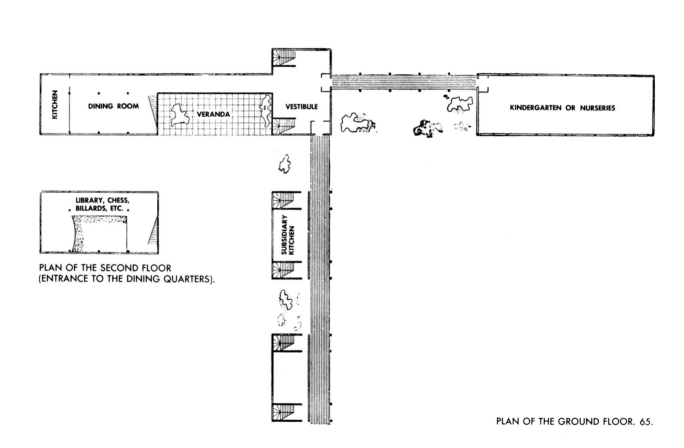

PLAN OF THE SECOND FLOOR
(ENTRANCE TO THE DINING QUARTERS).

PLAN OF THE GROUND FLOOR. 65.

1ST FLOOR

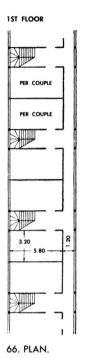

PER COUPLE

PER COUPLE

3.20
5.80
1.20

66. PLAN.

2-3 FLOOR

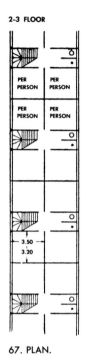

PER PERSON | PER PERSON

PER PERSON | PER PERSON

3.50
3.20

67. PLAN.

ROOF

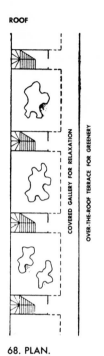

COVERED GALLERY FOR RELAXATION

OVER-THE-ROOF TERRACE FOR GREENERY

68. PLAN.

69. PLAN.

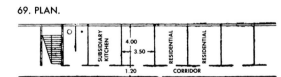

SUBSIDIARY KITCHEN

4.00
3.50

RESIDENTIAL

RESIDENTIAL

1.20   CORRIDOR

SCHEMATIC LAYOUT. 70.

DINING   DINING

RESIDENTIAL

NURSERY   KINDERGARTEN

VIEW AT GROUND LEVEL. 71.

72. GENERAL VIEW.

73. HOUSE OF THE SOVIETS IN MAKHACHKALA.[57]

74. SANATORIUM IN THE UKRAINE WHICH
LOOKS MORE LIKE A CREMATORIUM.[58]

11 THE CHOICE OF MATERIALS AND CONSTRUCTION METHODS

THIS ISN'T A PARADE—IT'S A WAR.
PUSHKIN, *THE LITTLE HOUSE IN KOLOMNA.*

All our contemporary construction takes on the character of completely unnecessary monumentality, it is calculated for an excessive durability. In part the term of the amortization is too long. Our buildings are in the highest degree antediluvian; the materials are weighty and expensive, which causes our buildings to be of extremely high cost and most cumbersome. Our houses remind one more of medieval castles than contemporary dwellings. Let us take two examples for illustration: The House of Soviets in Makhachkala (Dagestan) built in the form of a Genoese castle of the sixteenth century (Fig. 73) and either Professor Ginzburg's project for a contemporary apartment house (Fig. 76)—or our own proposal for house-communes (see Figs. 71–72). A quick look suffices to reveal the absurdity, extrav-

75. ACADEMICIAN ZHOLTOVSKII. THE GOSBANK BUILDING IN MOSCOW.
A MODEL OF THE MOST TASTELESS ECLECTICISM.[60]

agance, and senseless monumentality of the Dagestan construction. Examples of such a prodigal waste of materials are endless. It is enough to illustrate the Central Telegraph Building on Gor'kii Street,[59] the Gosbank building on Neglinnaia Street (Moscow) [Fig. 75], a large number of buildings in Novosibirsk, etc., etc.

Meanwhile, **we have, at present, full opportunity to build with the light and inexpensive materials which we possess in abundance.** For example, we have wood, a fine material for light framework construction, fibrolite (sawdust with magnesia cement), torfleum (peat), torfo-veneer, materials made from textile wastes, Nekrasov **organo-silicate blocks,**[61] scutched bricks, glass-slag hollow concrete blocks, and many others.

These light and inexpensive **materials make possible the widespread installation of factories to produce standardized parts for buildings so that only the finished parts, the blocks, etc. need be transported to the construction site.** The Nekrasov organo-silicate blocks would be especially good in this connection.

Therefore, **one of the most** important problems of today **must be to recognize the working out of a type of light construction,** the setting of necessary standards, the development of standardized parts for lighter buildings, **and the organization of a mass production of these parts.** Most expedient would be the creation of an experimental institute for dwelling construction, such as the Bauhaus at Dessau, where all our outstanding and advanced architectural and engineering talents would be concentrated in order to work out both the planning and the construction of socially meaningful architecture and its equipment.

In the establishment of this institution there must be consolidated all the construction experience which now is extremely dispersed and is not united by one single will.

It seems to me that this institute must also work out the problems of communal construction, including those of water supply and sewage. The latter is all the more important since we still are extremely con-

servative in our approach to this matter. It is sufficient to point out that we are hardly using at present the American method of **wooden water pipes and sewer systems** which has proven itself, although this type of installation is not new here and can be met with in many parts of the USSR, where it has been used both simply and inexpensively.

Besides this, we have the experience of having built for an electric station in the Caucasus an extensive pipe system out of wood which handles quite high pressures.

If we could solve this problem, we would be able to open up completely new possibilities in the matter of development of water supply and heating networks, as well as sewage disposal—all of which would be extremely simple and inexpensive. In addition, this would free many tons of metal which we are at present literally burying in the ground.

The same can be said for the covering of our buildings.

Composition paper [*tol*], **rubberoid,** and similar materials are rarely used by us. Meanwhile their lightness, nonflammability, comparative cheapness, and simplicity of installation make it possible to convert the many millions of tons of metal of our roofs into productive machinery.

●

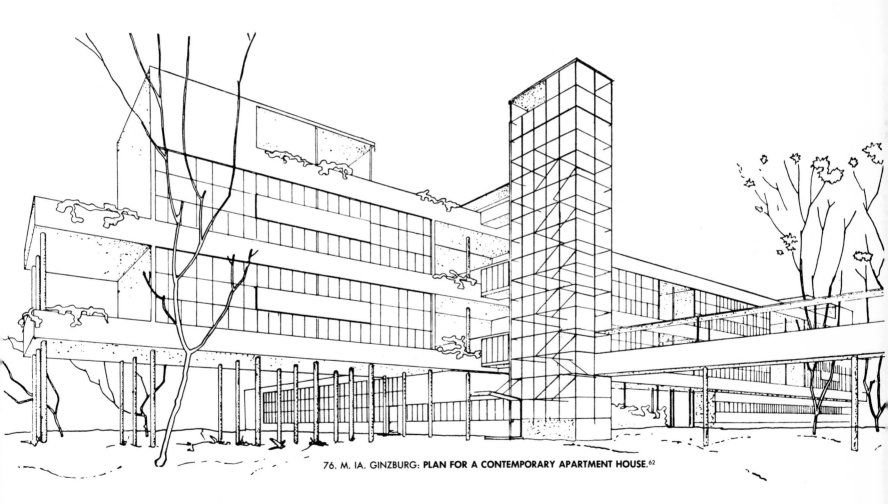

76. M. IA. GINZBURG: **PLAN FOR A CONTEMPORARY APARTMENT HOUSE.**[62]

THE BAUHAUS.[63] 77.

12 ARCHITECTURAL DESIGN

A few words on the architectural design of our construction. All these styles, Empires, Baroques, Renaissances, Gothics, and the like were very fine for their own epochs; they corresponded to the materials, ways of life, etc.

Our epoch—the epoch of the machine, of severe economy, new materials, new social relationships, and new forms of living—demands new architectural forms.

It would be an utterly senseless pursuit to try to invent these forms. **They must arise themselves as a result of the material and the structural content of the new buildings.** The architect's problem is to know how to find the most rational solution possible to the essence of the content of the

THE IDEAL IS NOTHING MORE THAN THE MATERIAL TRANSFORMED AND REDONE IN THE HUMAN HEAD.
K. MARX, *KAPITAL*[64]

building, while the form itself would be a logical consequence of this solution. Our architecture must, first and foremost, be honest, and **an honest solution to a correctly stated and correctly resolved problem cannot help but be beautiful.**

An intelligent structural solution needs no covering mask of decoration. A healthy face needs no powder.

The hopeless tedium of many plans for contemporary installations stems from the incorrect solution to architectural problems, not as a result of denial of decoration. Quite the contrary: not knowing how correctly to solve problems of architectural organization of the building and its construction causes many architects to hide their illiteracy and lack of ability behind the mask of "style" for which they either steal from their elders—calling this thievery by the delicate term "eclecticism"—or else they try to think up something "new" or "newest" in the way of style, accompanying their vices with noisy leftist phrases and twaddle about idealism, symbolism, and other such rubbish.

The Soviet settlement must be honest and simple in its forms—as the working class is honest and simple; **varied**—as life is varied; the parts that make up the buildings should be standardized **but not the buildings themselves; economical in the material and maintenance expended but not in their expanse and volume; joyous** as nature is joyous. Finally, they should be **comfortable, light, and hygienic.**

Lightness, expediency, simplicity, variety, cleanliness, a maximum of light— these are the qualities on which must be based the architectural design of Soviet construction.

MIES VAN DER ROHE.

SKYSCRAPER PROJECT.[65]   78.

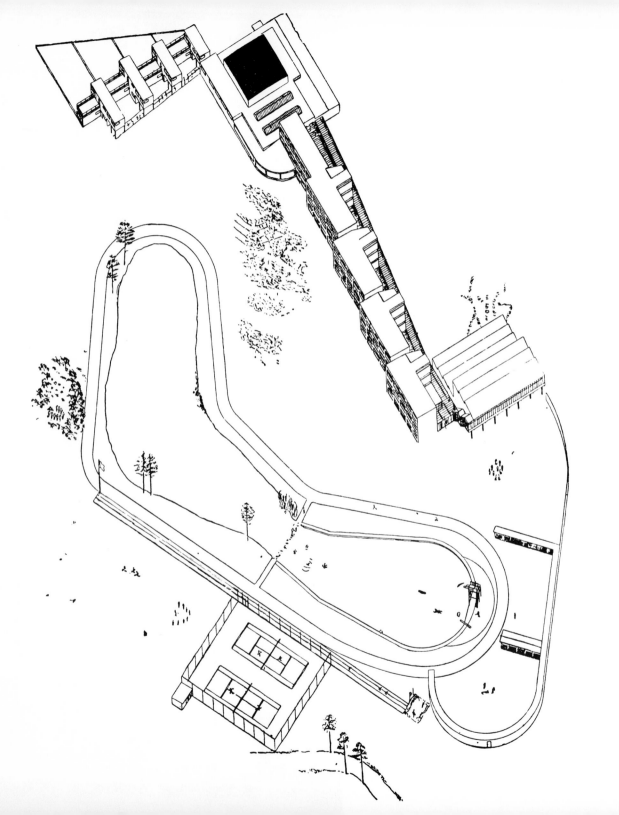

79.
CONTEMPORARY SCHOOL.
**AN EXAMPLE OF RATIONAL
PLANNING AND DESIGN.**[66]

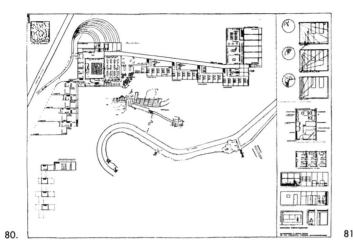

80.

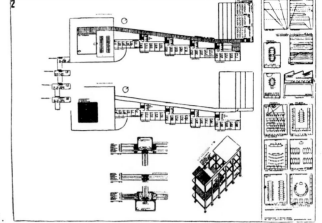

81.

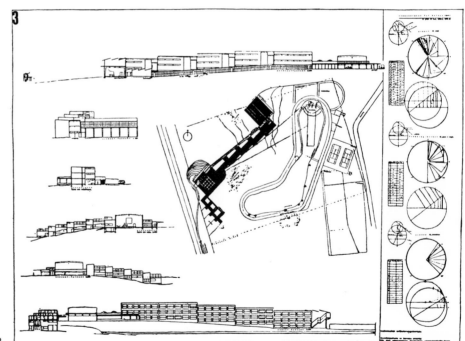

82.

**CONTEMPORARY SCHOOL.
AN EXAMPLE OF RATIONAL
PLANNING AND DESIGN.**

83.

85.

84.

LE CORBUSIER.
THE SLIDING WINDOW.[68]

87.

86.

88.

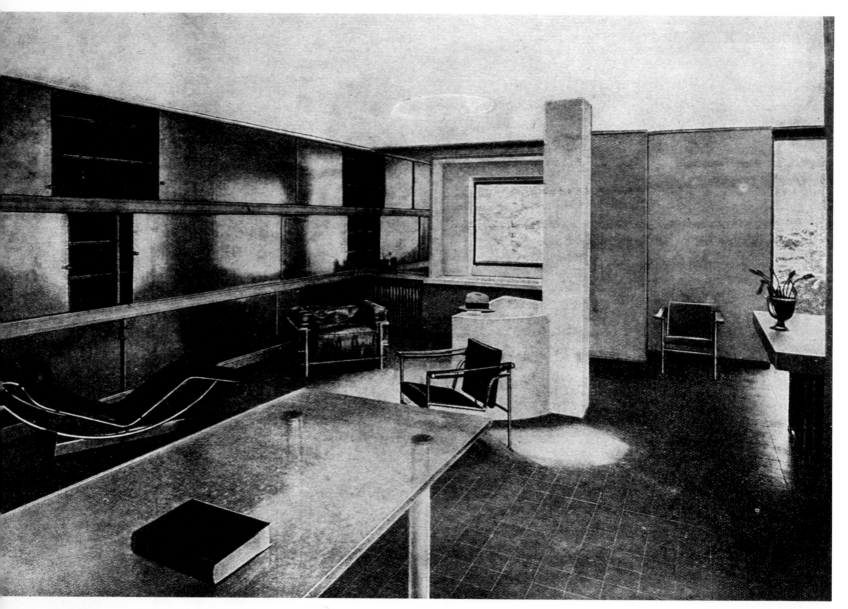

89. LE CORBUSIER. **LIBRARY**.[69]

LE CORBUSIER.
PEOPLE'S PALACE.[70]

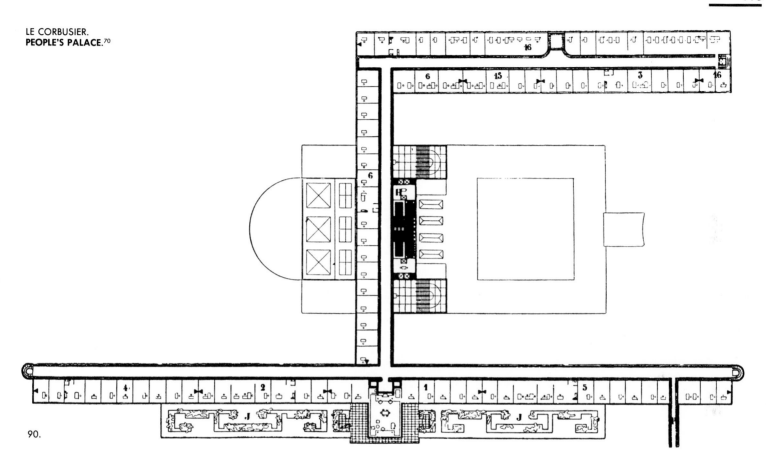

90.

91.

LE CORBUSIER. **TSENTROSOIUZ BUILDING**.[71] 92.

ARCHITECTURAL DESIGN
OF AN INSTITUTE.[72]

93.

94.

THE HIGHEST PRAISE MUST BE GIVEN TO THE COMMUNE PRECISELY BECAUSE IN ALL ITS ECONOMIC UNDERTAKINGS ITS "LIVE SOUL" WAS BASED NOT ON ANY PRINCIPLES BUT ON SOLID PRACTICAL DEMANDS.

F. ENGELS

13 COMPARATIVE COSTS OF CONSTRUCTION [73]

We have already noted that the organization of a socialized way of servicing the population leads new cadres into productive labor. At the present time Gosplan RSFSR has made a rather thorough accounting of the population of the workers' settlement at the Magnitogorsk industrial combine.

These calculations yield the following picture.

The general number of workers employed in the industrial combine is taken as 11,400. This number of workers in the future will be almost doubled, since at the present time the increase in volume of the productive task of the combine has already been predetermined. However, this change will hardly influence our calculations, since all other figures will increase in proportion to the increase in the number of workers.

Assuming this number employed in production at Magnitogorsk—both workers and service personnel **resident in settlements of the usual type**—it will be necessary to have about 3,500 workers and service personnel employed in servicing the soviet, communal, trade, and similar activities and institutions. Taking into account that the average family composition for the Union SSR, according to TsSU, consists of: for metal workers 3.7–3.8, for service personnel 3.6–3.7, and single persons comprise 12–14% in this branch of production—we arrive at the conclusion that **the whole population of the workers' settlement at Magnitogorsk will be from 49,500 to 51,000 people.** This number of inhabitants is the minimum, since in analogous settlements in the Urals (Motovilikha, Votkinskii Plant, et al.) the composition of families of the inhabitants varies from 3.8 to 4.1, which further raises the population by 10%, i.e., to 55,000 people.

Taking a minimal figure of the population of Magnitogorsk under conditions of usual construction at 50,000 people, we will need a total living space:
At a norm of 9 m³ per person: 450,000 m³
at a norm of 6 m³ per person: 300,000 m³

Using a relationship of volume to living area established by VSNKh as 8, we will have a building volume of:
At a norm of 9 m³ per person:

3,600,000 m³

at a norm of 6 m³ per person:

2,400,000 m³

At a cost per m³ considered normal for the Ural area as 20 r., **the general cost of construction for residential buildings of the usual type for the Magnitogorsk settlements will consist of:**
At a norm of 9 m³ per person:

72,000,000 r.

at a norm of 6 m³ per person:

48,000,000 r.

If, however, in building Magnitogorsk we could immediately assure the population of all basic forms of socialized services for its most pressing needs, that would allow us to attract a large sector of the employable dependent population into productive work and service institutions and significant activities, and the picture would be entirely different.

Thus, according to the Gosplan calculations of 11,400 workers and service personnel occupied in production, in the servicing there will be employed from 6,500 to 7,000, and the entire dependent population will be from 18,000 to 18,500 as against 15,000 dependents in a settlement of the usual sort.

However, due to the fact that a very significant part of the employable population is usually tied up in domestic tasks, with **socialized services,** there will be the opportunity to draw this sector into production and service activities and institutions, and the **overall number of inhabitants of the settlement would drop to 33,500— 31,500 people.** Moreover, due to the peculiarities of the metallurgic industry, this would leave only 1,500 employable people unoccupied, the labor of whom could be put to use in the future in subsidiary agricultural activities.

In this case, given a norm of $8\frac{1}{2}$–9 m³ and 1–$1\frac{1}{2}$ m³ of additional space for service accommodations (cafeteria, library), we would have a usable area relationship of a cubature of 5, resulting in 50—55 m³ of residential space per person.

From the same [Gosplan] calculation indicated above we can calculate the cubature for children's institutions (except for schools, which are excluded from the accounts of both variants).[74]

In this way for a maximum of 33,000 inhabitants in a settlement with socialized services, we will need a maximum of 1,815,000 m³ of all types of residential construction (including nurseries, kindergartens, boarding schools, cafeterias, libraries, etc.) at a maximum cost of 36,300,000 r. at a price of 20 r. per m³ as in the first usual variant. This cost can undoubtedly be significantly lowered through standardization of the dwelling unit, etc.

Thus we see that **with identical norms and with identical costs of construction, even without full usage of the total able and working population, the very greatest expense for residential construction of the village with socialized services will be 2 times less than** [i.e., $\frac{1}{2}$ as much as] **the least possible expense for residential construction of settlements of the usual type.**

If the usual settlement is constructed at the least imaginable expense for 6 m³ per person, even then the settlement with socialized servicing will cost 25% less than the "usual" in spite of the fact that there will be almost twice as much available living space per person. ●

In these accounts for both the first and second alternatives, expenses are excluded for administrative, commercial, communal, school, hospital, transportation, and other construction. But, here again, in the settlement with socialized services, much less expense is necessary for construction; thus, for example, in this instance, all expenses are eliminated for the construction of specialized buildings for nurseries, maternity and children's homes, orphan asylums, cafeterias, a large number of commercial buildings, etc.

Moreover, the volume of these structures will be reduced, for instance in hospitals, administration buildings, etc. due to the fewer number of inhabitants and better living conditions.

We draw on the example of the construction figures for Magnitogorsk because they give the most pessimistic accounts for a settlement with socialized services of the living needs of its population:

1) labor conditions in the heavy-metal industry are least auspicious with respect to female labor, which leads to the impossibility of full employment of the able-bodied population, leaving a remainder of unoccupied but employable persons of 1,500;

2) the fact that Magnitogorsk is being built in an isolated site does not present the possibilities which would be available, for example in Stalingrad, through use of an already existing dependent labor force;

3) the climatic conditions of Magnitogorsk demand the adoption of the types of

---

● For detailed accounts by Gosplan, see Appendix.

construction that are connected by heated corridors which necessitate 5 m³ for each square meter of living area. Under other conditions (for example, in the Crimea, Northern Caucasus, in the Transcaucasus, Turkmenistan, Uzbekistan, Southern Ukraine, etc.) it is possible to use the corridorless system of construction (for example, that proposed by Stroikom RSFSR) which would lower this coefficient to 3.2, i.e., would lower construction costs by 25–35% besides the resultant lessening of costs through lighter construction, the simplification of heating installations, etc.

Thus from these Gosplan figures, it is evident that the construction of dwellings of the socialist type will require significantly less means than construction of the usual type.

This fact has tremendous significance in that it decisively refutes the major argument of the conservative elements of our establishment, who maintain that this type of construction is beyond our means. It is easy to see that this argument is based exclusively on a lack of familiarity with the question. Obviously such figures need experimental verification. However, they show such a "margin of safety" that they can undoubtedly be considered entirely realistic.

14

THE MAJOR ITEMS
OF THE BUDGET [75]

It is obvious that a necessary condition for instituting socialized services for the needs of the population is the availability of a corresponding material basis. In the previous chapter we showed that as regards the costs of capital construction the question can be considered completely resolved since, all things being equal, construction intended for socialized services for the population needs will be at least twice as economical [i.e., cost $\frac{1}{2}$ as much] as the usual. As for the capability of the population to meet current costs of socialized child education, the answer lies in the accounts given below.

If we take conditions in Moscow, where we have the highest salaries and highest product costs and consequently the highest outlay for upkeep of children's institutions, we have the following results.

Per 1,000 inhabitants of Moscow there are:

Children to age 3 years	91.2
Children from age 4 to 7	58.6
Children from age 8 to 14	86.2
Youths from age 15 to 17.........	52.3
Able-bodied population.............	667.7
Unemployable and elderly	44.0
Total	1,000.0

From these figures we find that per 100 able-bodied inhabitants of Moscow there are:

Children to age 3 years	13.7
Children from age 4 to 7	8.7
Children from age 8 to 14	12.9
Youths from age 15 to 17...........	7.8
Unemployable and elderly	6.4
Total	49.5

Using these figures for the Moscow population we will arrive at the following expenses for each 100 employable adults.

1. Nurseries. The maximum expense for the complete maintenance of a child in the nursery under best conditions including all overhead expenses, according to data of Narkomzdrav RSFSR, is about 60 r. per month. This norm is almost three times above the present actual outlay and is calculated for the complete maintenance of children for 24 hours a day with the largest service staff, consisting entirely of hired help (who have no other social responsibilities).

Given the average number of children in this age group as 13.7 per 100 able-bodied residents, the total expense for them will be 822 r. or 8 r. 22 k. for each one.

Part of these expenses are already covered by social security out of the monthly budget of FUBR; for the sake of simplicity we will take into account these expenses in our general conclusion.

2. Kindergartens. The cost of complete maintenance of children in kindergarten, according to data of Narkompros RSFSR, is about 50 r. per month including all types of services. This rate of expense, as with nurseries, is significantly higher than that of the present.

Per 100 able-bodied inhabitants there are 8.7 children of this age (from 4 to 7 inclusive) which give an average cost of maintenance of 435 r. per month or 4 r. 35 k. for each such adult.

3. School dormitories of first and second forms. The cost of complete maintenance of children of school age (from 8 to 14 inclusive), according to data of Narkompros is (excluding instruction) about 40 r. per month.

Per 100 able-bodied inhabitants there are 12.9 children of this age with a consequent average cost of 516 r. per month or 5 r. 16 k. for each such adult.

4. Dormitories for the third form (from 15 to 17 inclusive). With the average number of youths in this group at 7.8 and the cost of maintenance for each of about 40 r. per month, the total sum of expenses will be 312 r. or 3 r. 12 k. per one such adult.

Thus the expenses for socialized education of children and youths given according to Moscow figures per 100 able-bodied persons can be expressed in the following figures:

	In Nurseries	In Kindergarten	In Dormitories	Youths (in technical schools)	Totals
1. The children per hundred able-bodied inhabitants	13.7	8.7	12.9	7.8	43.1
2. Full cost of maintenance for one child	60 r.	50 r.	40 r.	40 r.	48 r. [approx.]
3. Same for all children	822 r.	435 r.	516 r.	312 r.	2,085 r.
4. For each able-bodied person	8.22 r.	4.35 r.	5.16 r.	3.12 r.	20.85 r.

From this sum (20 r. 85 k.) must be subtracted expenses already covered otherwise at present:

1. Social Security expenditures. These expenses compiled for Moscow at present (1929–30) are about 5,000,000 r. per year or 50 k. per month for each taxable adult. This sum must be increased by $1\frac{1}{2}$ since under socialized services the number of working adults (i.e., those insured) per 100 children will increase by 50–60%. In this way, each insured individual will pay:................................. 75 k.

2. Budget expenditures of FUBR, cooperatives, etc. (excluding expenses for construction, stipends, etc.) come in 1929–30 to about 20,000,000 r. per year or about 2 r. per month for those insured, without considering the increase in funds available due to the rise in number of workers (i.e., those insured), but taking into account the rise it would consist of 50–60% .... 3 r.

3. Stipends to youths and profits from apprentice workshops which must at least ensure financial independence of this group of youths (from 15 to 17); this will cost each insured individual .... 3 r. 12 k.

4. Products of training in- stitutions of the second form out of an outlay of 10 r. per month for each child of this group, or for each insured..........1 r. 29 k.

Total 8 r. 16 k.

Thus expenses not covered at the present time for each employable member of the adult population of Moscow, taking into account the increase resulting from the growth of the employed (i.e., insured people) will be................................ 12 r. 69 k. which must be procured in order to cover all current expenses for complete education of all children and youths up through age 17.

Three sources must be tapped for this sum. First the fund of socialized wages must be increased by raising the rate of insurance fees by a certain percentage (through social insurance) for living needs; then normal growth of the monthly budget will systematically increase the worker's portion of his expenses for these needs; and finally through partial payment by parents, depending on their wages and the size of their family.

It is easy to see, therefore, that practically speaking, **from the financial viewpoint hardly anything remains to be done by us to create a solid material basis for socialized education of children throughout Moscow. The whole thing is only a matter of organizing our possibilities and capabilities.**

In the provinces, as regards the group of insured population we have almost the same picture (the expenses of social insurance and budget are lower, but the wages, the prices of products, etc. are lower still).

Of course the village presents a different scene. There remains an enormous amount of work to be done there on the reconstruction of agricultural bases, which is the only means of creating the conditions for a corresponding transformation of mutual social aid into a solid socialization of partial income from the population that would be analogous to social insurance. The **solution** to this problem—**the problem of socialist reconstruction of agriculture—is an essential premise for the institution of full socialization of the living needs of the village population.** At the present time, in the countryside it is only possible to create a few nuclei and connecting links as a premise of the future system of a new way of life, in the form of summer nurseries, institutions for orphans, and so on. **Only by means of increasing the growth of the people's wages and productive labor on the basis of a new organization of agriculture and its mechanization, is a solution conceivable to the problem of reconstructing the village way of life.** This must be recalled to comrades who think that only by organizational measures is it possible to skip the hurdles and difficulties that stand on the road to reconstruction of a new way of life in the country.[76]

Cost accounting of socialized feeding, laundries, and other types of communal services for the population need not even be mentioned here since it is obvious that large-scale production will always be many times more economic than a small-scale one. The whole question reduces itself to the matter of organizational possibilities, the difficulties of which can by no means be underestimated. Therefore we recommend a certain caution and consistency without which the whole idea of the organization of the new way of life might be discredited.

In establishing an expanding net of socialized feeding and laundries at the present stage we must nevertheless envisage the possibility of individual food preparation and the possibility of individual laundries which in no way signifies a retaining of the system of construction of small family apartments. While discarding compulsion in instituting the new way of life, we should by no means preserve the old way of life. On the contrary, **all our strength, all attention must be directed toward the creation of a real material basis for the new way of life.**

The form of organization of the dwelling with its subsidiary accommodations is one of the most important elements in the organization of the services for the population. This circumstance must definitely be considered by both our builders and planners as well as by the Soviet public. **Only by achieving an awareness of the organizational role of the habitation in the goal of reconstructing our way of life and consequently in all aspects of our life by the widest possible masses of workers of the USSR will we be able to find the most correct solution to the problem of a new settlement of humanity and the shortest and most rational way to create the material basis for building a new socialist world.**

The correct posing and proper solution of the problem of industrial and residential construction in the USSR must create **"such conditions for work and living for the working class, which will give us the opportunity to nurture a new generation of workers, healthy and vital, able to raise the might of our Soviet country to deserving heights and to bodily defend her against encroachment by the enemy"** (J. Stalin, speech at the XVI Party Congress).

This is why the problem of organizing the battle for the new way of life must be one of the foremost of our problems.

"Party organizations must render every possible assistance to this movement and direct it ideologically. Soviets, trade unions, and cooperatives must assume practical solutions to the problems connected with this goal. It is necessary that we observe the various undertakings of workers participating in the reconstruction of the way of life with greatest attention, thoroughly studying the sprouting of the new, and in every way assist their realization in life." (From the resolution of the TsK VKP(b) [Central Committee of the Bolshevik Communist Party] Congress of 16 May 1930).

APPENDIXES

ACCOUNT OF GOSPLAN RSFSR ON THE NUMBER OF INHABITANTS FOR THE CITY OF MAGNITOGORSK UNDER CONDITIONS OF SOCIALIZED SERVICES FOR THE POPULATION'S NEEDS.[77]

I

a) Occupied on regular schedule in the *kombinat:*

Workers .... 9,910 persons
Service personnel .... 1,491 "
Total ....11,401 "

b) Conditions of production allow hiring of the following:

	Workers		Service Personnel		
	persons	%	persons	%	Total
Men	6,937	70	895	60	7,832
Women	2,973	30	596	40	3,569
Total	9,910	—	1,491	—	11,401

II

a) Involved in production that men only can do ....70% 6,937 persons
For these there are usually (according to TsSU) women.4.6%   319 "

   Basic cadre of workers ....7,256 "

b) Of the men, single (data of TsSU) ....12–13%   853 persons
Heads of families 6,084 persons, total..................................6,937 "
Of the women: single (according to TsSU)................28%   90 "
Married 72%—229 persons, total .... 319 "

   In all single 943 persons, married 6,313 persons, Total..7,256 "

III

Average composition of the family:

Men 3.8 persons × 6,084..= 23,119 persons
Women 3.2 persons × 229..=   743 "
Single..   943 "

   Total workers' population including families................ 24,895 "

IV

a) (see paragraph I) service personnel—male—involves
   only 60% .... 895 persons
For them, there are usually 25–26% women .... 233 "

   Basic cadre of service personnel ....1,128 "

b) Of male service personnel: single 13.5–14%..................... 125 persons
married—770 persons, total.. 895 "
Of female service personnel: single 37%........................... 86 "
married—147 persons, total.. 233 "

   In all single 211 persons, married 917 persons, total.....1,128 "

V

Average composition of the family:

Men 3.8 × 770.. = 2,926 persons
Women 73.2 × 147.. =   470 "
Single... 211 "

   Total .... 3,607 "

VI

Total population, connected with production:

		Of that number— independents	Of that number— dependents
Workers and members of their families	24,805	7,256	17,549
Service personnel and members of their families	3,607	1,128	2,479
Total	28,412	8,384	20,028

VII

According to accounting records, preliminary regular studies of the public, socio-cultural, and servicing institutions show that there will be about 5,480 vacancies of which 1,430 must be filled by men (with consequent female vacancies at 4,050).

Of the 1,430 men, 14% of single men will be drawn in from the outside, i.e., 200, and 1,230 married.

Family coefficient 3.8 ....4,674 persons
Single .... 200 "
Total...4,874 "

VIII

	Of the total population	Of that number— independent	Of that number— dependents
Connected with production	28,412 persons	8,384	20,028
Connected with services	4,874 persons	1,430	3,444
Total	33,286 persons	9,814	23,472

But there were 11,401 vacancies, 8,384 were hired in connection with production, leaving 3,017
But there were 5,480 vacancies, 1,430 were hired in connection with service, leaving 4,050

Total ... 16,881 [minus those hired:] 9,814 [,leaving] 7,067

Available vacancies to the number 7,067 must be taken up by dependents.

Therefore we have the following population structure:
total 33,286,   independent 16,881,   dependent 16,405

IX

According to TsSU figures, the composition of the families of metal workers and service personnel, by age:

	Single	Heads of Families	Members of the Family up to Age 16	16–59	60 or Older
Working men	893	6,084	7,398	8,250	1,387
Working women	90	229	260	225	29
Service men	125	770	878	1,132	146
Service women	86	147	122	168	33
Assistance men	200	1,230	1,392	1,838	234
Total	1,354	8,460	10,040	11,603	1,729

Overall number 33,286 persons

Transferring the dependent population within the age group 16–59 (11,603 persons), into available vacancies (7,067), we will have an excess of 4,536 people of which only about one thousand will be occupied with servicing of the housing; the youngest group (16–19) will be freed from work for study in the mining technical school (440 persons) and the 10-year school (500 persons); we must allow 3% unemployable for various reasons (illness, etc.)—about one thousand persons.

There is a remaining reserve of 1,496 of unused labor force, the labor of whom could be organized in craft-industry cooperatives and workshops, on the nearby state farms [sovkhozy], family garden allotments [ogoroda], etc.

All the figures are based on maximum coefficients. Thus, the quantity of single persons could be increased, which would lower the population by about 1,000–1,500 persons; the female composition of the population occupied in production could be raised by 500, which would further decrease the population by 1,500, etc.

CONCERNING THE WORK OF RECONSTRUCTING OUR WAY OF LIFE
RESOLUTION OF THE TsK VKP (b) [CENTRAL COMMITTEE
OF THE BOLSHEVIK COMMUNIST PARTY]
16 MAY 1930

The successful course of socialist reconstruction—industrialization of the country in particular—creates at the present moment the necessary foundations for systematic work on the reconstruction of our way of life along socialist principles. The enthusiasm of the working masses for the fastest possible completion of the Five-Year Plan begins to take hold on our way of life. In a number of undertakings there have arisen everyday life brigades who enter into social competition with the cooperatives and who take over the direction and control of socialized feeding of children's nurseries, of kindergartens, etc.

Party organizations must render every possible assistance to this movement and direct it ideologically. Soviets, trade unions, and cooperatives must assume practical solutions to the problems connected with this goal. It is necessary that we observe the various undertakings of workers participating in the reconstruction of the way of life with greatest attention, thoroughly studying the sprouting of the new, and in every way assisting their realization in life.

The Central Committee notices that together with the growing movement toward a socialist way of life there are quite baseless, half-fantastic, therefore extremely dangerous experimental efforts on the part of individual comrades (Sabsovich, Larin in part, and others).[78] They with "one jump" would skip across those obstacles on the road to socialist reconstruction of our way of life that have their roots on the one hand in the economic and cultural backwardness of the country and on the other in the present necessity for the maximum concentration of all resources toward the quickest means of industrialization of the country; the latter alone will create the real material basis for a radical change of our way of life. To such attempts of certain workers, hiding their opportunistic character under "leftist slogans," are related the projects which have appeared recently in print: projects for the replanning of existing cities and the reconstruction of new ones, entirely at the cost of the state, with full and immediate socialization of all aspects of the way of life of the workers: feeding, residence, education of children with their separation from their parents, elimination of relations between the members of the families, and administrative suppression of individual preparation of food, etc. The implementation of these dangerous utopian principles, which take no account of the material resources of the country and the degree of preparation of the population, would lead to a colossal waste of resources and a cruel discreditation of the very idea of socialist reconstruction of our way of life.

Therefore the TsK resolves:

1) To propose that the SNK of the Union within 15 days prepare directions about the regulations for construction of workers' settlements and separate residences for the workers. These instructions must take into account the development of collective servicing of the way of life of the workers (laundries, baths, factory kitchens, children's institutions, cafeterias, etc.) in cities and in settlements which are either being built or are already extant.

2) To ensure a sufficient green belt between the industrial and the living zones in the construction of workers' settlements at new major enterprises (Stalingrad, Dneprostroi, Magnitogorsk, Chelyabinsk, etc.), to provide roads and communication, and to supervise the equipping of these settlements with water systems, electric lighting, bathing facilities, laundries, communal cafeterias, children's institutions, clubs, schools, and medical care. In new construction there must be maximum sanitary conditions and hygienic facilities, and it is also necessary to take all measures to ensure the lowest construction costs.

3) To direct the attention of all party organizations to the necessity, in connection with these tasks, of significantly strengthening efforts toward a maximum mobilization of the energy of the population itself in residential construction, through residence-construction cooperation.

4) To mandate the Narkomtrud USSR and VTsSPS together with the cooperatives, to take urgent measures to ensure regulation and amplification of the financing of the reconstruction of the way of life in view of the present lack of cooperation between financial organizations and professional trade union organizations of the various socio-cultural institutions.

5) To give the commission on the reconstruction of our way of life at the NK RKI USSR the responsibility of implementing extant resolutions.

6) To propose that SNK issue a directive to the VSNKh USSR to expand, beginning with the present fiscal year, production of equipment for services for the working class (factory kitchens, mechanized laundries, communal cafeterias, social dining rooms, etc.) and to assess the question of the increase in the financing of measures for the reconstruction of our way of life.

CONTENTS

GLAVLIT NO. A—71188

PUBLISHED BY THE STATE PUBLISHING HOUSE RSFSR IN A QUANTITY OF 7,000 COPIES.
A 13. NO. 40065

SETUP, LAYOUT, PRINTING, AND BINDING BY THE "RED PROLETARIAT" PRINTING HOUSE.
MOSCOW, KRASNOPROLETARSKAIA [RED PROLETARIAN ST.], 16.
ORDER NO. 1229, 7 PRINTED SHEETS.

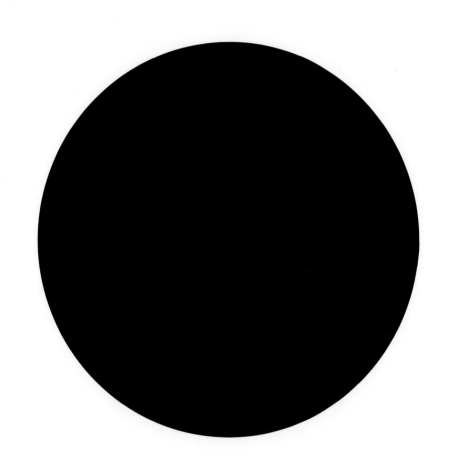

OF THESE NOTES, THE FOLLOWING HAVE BEEN TAKEN FROM THE MANUSCRIPT OF THE TRANSLATION THAT ARTHUR SPRAGUE LEFT: 2, 3, 5, 6, 8, 11, 18–21, 23, 25, 26, 28–32, 35, 36, 40–42, 57–60, 64, 66, 70—72. OUR NOTES 9 AND 27 ALSO INCORPORATE HIS MATERIAL — G. R. C.

NOTES TO TRANSLATION

1. *Problema Stroi*tel'stva *Sotsialisticheskikh Gorod*ov. See "Sotsgorod" in Glossary. The word *stroitel'stvo* can signify various professional usages in English and, depending on the context, is in our text translated as "planning," "construction," or "city building."

2. An Aleksei Petrovich Smirnov (b. 1899) was one of the first Soviet archaeologists to do sociological and economic research on the Volga Bulgarians and the Finnish feudal cities. See *Bol'shaia Sovetskaia Entsiklopediia* (*Larger Soviet Encyclopedia, BSE*), 2nd ed. (1956), XXXIX, p. 405.

3. N. L. Meshcheriakov (1865–1942), from 1920 to 1938 chief editor of the *Malaia Sovetskaia Entsiklopediia* (*Shorter Soviet Encyclopedia*) and chairman of the board of the *BSE*. See the latter, 2nd ed. (1954), XXVII, p. 403. As a theorist of the socialist city, Meshcheriakov suffered attacks in the later period of reaction along with Miliutin, Okhitovich, and others. This came at the hands of Svetlov and Gornyi in their piece, "The socialist city in a society without classes" (1934).

4. Nicholas Barbon (c. 1640–98), English economist, as quoted by Karl Marx in his footnotes to the opening paragraphs of *Das Kapital*. Marx printed the following extract from Barbon's *A Discourse concerning Coining the New Money Lighter*, London, 1696 (pp. 2, 3): "Desire implies Want; it is the Appetite of the Mind, and as natural as Hunger to the Body. . . . The greatest Number (of things) have their value from supplying the Wants of the Mind." Barbon also wrote on trade and on the economics of building, although we do not know whether Miliutin was aware of this. The exploits of Barbon, an entrepreneur involved in rebuilding London after the Great Fire, are described by J. Summerson in *Architect and Building News*, CXLIX, 15 Jan. 1937, pp. 86–89. Barbon's publications are not actually as rare as is suggested in Summerson's article, existing in several editions in the Columbia University libraries, for instance.

5. Preface to the first edition of 1867. The remark "Le mort saisit le vif" follows this.

6. Kitaigorod: the old market to the west of the Kremlin, which once included what is now Red Square; in Russian, literally "Chinatown." It is, however, more probably derived from the Tartar word for fortress, *Kitai*, than from the Russian word for China, *Kitai*.

7. The XVI Party Congress opened on 26 June 1930. Miliutin cites it more than once, indicating that his book was completed in the latter part of 1930.

8. S. I. Syrtsov, a Communist official for many years, was elected to the Politburo in July 1930 and expelled therefrom in December of the same year for criticizing the new industrialization (he called it "eyewash") and for having termed the Stalingrad Tractor Plant, which figures so largely in this book, a "Potemkin village." See Leonard Schapiro, *The Communist Party of the Soviet Union* (1960), pp. 390–91. Quoting Syrtsov may have proved a source of embarrassment to Miliutin after the appearance of his book.

9. Probably Tommaso Campanella (1568–1639) whose *Civitas Solis* of 1623 described an ideal communist utopia. This work had significant influence on Lenin and Lunacharskii and is widely read in the Soviet Union. According to Lunacharskii, Lenin took his idea of creating an inspiring and instructive artistic environment for the citizenry from a description in Campanella. The conversation between Lenin and Lunacharskii is described and quoted in Hellmut Lehmann-Haupt, *Art under a Dictatorship*, NYC, Oxford, 1954, p. 227. The exclamation points in parentheses (!) are Miliutin's. They are used as signs of astonishment or, as inserted in brackets in the quotation from Lunacharskii that follows, sarcasm.

10. Regarding Miliutin and Lunacharskii see Introduction, note 27.

11. Quoted from Goethe by Engels in *Zur Wohnungsfrage*. See F. Engels, *The Housing Question*, Marxist-Leninist Library, XXIII, NYC, International Publishers, 1935, p. 96.

12. That is, in the USSR. See note 41.

13. This quotation from Lenin was a favorite with the group. Ginzburg cited it in his correspondence with Le Corbusier in 1930, as recounted in Kopp, *Town and Revolution* p. 254.

14. Close-up of the model (1930) of the Plan Voisin of 1925 for Paris.

15. Marx's statement continued: "by a more equable distribution of the population over the countryside."

16. See note 11. Oddly enough, Kaganovich quoted a similar passage from Engels the following year to prove the exactly opposite position.

17. This analysis of the difference between capitalist and communist cities was apparently current; Ernst May used almost the same phraseology in his "Der Bau der Städte in der UdSSR," in *Das Neue Russland* (1931), which was a report he had given twice in Germany that year about his experiences in the Soviet Union.

18. This chapter was translated into Italian in Ceccarelli *La costruzione della città sovietica 1929–31*, pp. 68–80, as far as our p. 73 "machines in them."

19. *v svoem navoze:* literally, "in their own dung" or "excrement."

20. *potochnyi:* usually given as a method of conveyor belt production. To Americans this is Ford's familiar "assembly line" and is so translated here.

21. i.e., as industrial workers.

22. Night soil is still extensively used as fertilizer in many countries; we are one of the few cultures in history that has not exploited human and industrial wastes. Miliutin was aware of the benefits of organic cycling in the agricultural process. Kaganovich in his 1931 Bolshevik Party Plenum Address (in Kaganovich, *Socialist Reconstruction of Moscow and other Cities in the USSR*, p. 44) said, "these sewage beds must be transformed into soil fertilization beds. This can produce a large quantity of vegetables."

23. *Kapital* (translated from the third German edition), Moscow, n.d., I, p. 484. Marx relates this idea to the factory system and apparently derives his wording from Robert Owen, *Observations on the Effects of the Manufacturing System*, London, 1817, which he included in the bibliography of *Kapital*.

24. This is not found in English editions of the *Manifesto*.

25. *gorsel'sovet:* A soviet combining the functions of both town and village organiza-

tions.

26. *internat:* dormitory for school children; also translated as boarding school.

27. It is curious that in his emphasis on efficiency, Miliutin does not discuss the tremendous economic significance of the USSR's extensive inland waterway system (except for a passing comment in connection with his Stalingrad plan—see p. 71). He sees water as useful for attractive recreational spots and for its hygienic advantages at a time when one of the major thrusts of the Five-Year Plan was to develop water transport as a supplement to the overburdened rail system. No quays or docks seem to be provided in his plans. See also Introduction, note 54.

28. This appears to be the plan given in G. B. Minervin (see Bibl.), p. 16, Fig. 3, as that of the "engineer" R. Brilling. There was a competition for the design of Magnitogorsk in 1929 but no serious work took place until S. Chernyshev and Ernst May went to the site in the late fall of 1930. The American engineering firm of Arthur G. McKee (Russian *Mak-ki*) was also involved in the planning of Magnitogorsk, and a contract for drawings was drawn up and signed in New York in 1930.

Professor Samuel Lieberstein of Temple University is doing interesting, as yet unpublished work on the Ural-Kuznetsk Combine.

29. This is a schematic representation of the plan drawn up for Magnitogorsk by I. I. Leonidov in 1930. See p. 23.

30. This is apparently the plan referred to in Minervin, p. 16, as "urbanistic." It splits the town in half, placing industry on one bank and a ribbonlike residential strip on the other; it was planned for 50,000 inhabitants. It is discussed further in *Stroitel'naia Promyshlennost'* (*Construction Industry*), 1930, No. 3, pp. 195–99. It is hard to understand Miliutin's approbation—with the exception of his approval of the linear residential area—since travel to and from work would necessitate crossing the river.

31. *Stalingradstroi:* construction committee for the project. Stalingrad, formerly Tsaritsyn, is now Volgograd.

32. For comparable aerial-view-oriented thinking in Russia see Kasimir Malevich, *The Non-Objective World*, Chicago, Theobald, 1959 (originally published as *Die Gegendstandslose Welt*, Bauhausbuch 11, Munich, 1927). Illustrations 28–35 give "The environment (reality) which stimulates the Suprematist." Paul Scheerbart and Bruno Taut had popularized these ideas.

33. Nizhegorod, short for Nizhninovgorod, renamed Gor'kii in 1932.

34. The Russian text here erroneously cites "Fig. 9."

35. *xylolite:* an artificial "woodstone."

36. *tol':* tar paper, roofing felt or roofing pasteboard.

36a. This chapter appeared, translated and somewhat abbreviated in "V.O.K.S.", II, No. 2, 1931, pp. 29–31, and extracts are also printed in App. 8 of Kopp, *Town and Revolution*.

37. The standard English translations of the German original vary somewhat from this.

38. Kaganovich also quotes this in his Bolshevik Party Plenum Address of 1931 which is discussed in our Introduction. It is from "A Great Beginning" of 1919.

39. From the *Communist Manifesto*. Again, the standard English translations of the German vary somewhat from Miliutin's quotation.

40. Compare Edward Bellamy, *Looking Backward, 2000–1887*, Modern Library, 1951, p. 104: "We have a separate grade, unconnected with the others,—a sort of invalid corps, the members of which are provided with a light class of tasks fitted to their strength. All our sick in mind and body . . . belong to this invalid corps . . ." And futher on, Dr. Leete snaps, "There is no such thing in a civilized society as self support."

41. The reference is most probably to Leonard Moiseevich Sabsovich, an originator of the

"sleeping cabin" theory. A rabid collectivist, he had written a book entitled *Sotsialicheskie Goroda* (*Socialist Cities*), published by the Moscow State Technical Publishing House the same year as Miliutin's. He belonged to a militant organization called VARNITSO, an abbreviation for Vsesoiuznaia Assotsiatsiia Rabotnikov Nauki i Tekniki Sodeistviia Sotsialisticheskomu Stroitel' stvu (The All-Union Association of Workers in Science and Technology Working toward Socialist Reconstruction). This is a title artificially chosen so that its initials would spell *varnitso* (boiler). Sabsovich wanted to collectivize everything immediately and to eliminate not only the difference between town and country and the difference in work status between men and women, but the difference between mental and physical work. He wanted to "change the face of the earth, change mankind" (*SSSR cherez 10 Let* [1930], p. 117). On Sabsovich see also Kopp, *Town and Revolution*, passim, and our Introduction, p. 28.

41a. This is the bedroom designed for Erwin Piscator by Marcel Breuer in Berlin, 1927.

42. This project (Figs. 24–30) was published by Ginzburg and Barshch as part of their "Green City" in *SA*, 1930, No. 1-2.

43. It should be noted that Miliutin also designed a nursery building. See Introduction, pp. 31–32.

44. Narkompros was Miliutin's parent organization. See Glossary.

45. El Lissitzky in his *Russland* (1930) describes a project by A. Nikolski that also emphasized single-story construction (p. 52 in the MIT Press edition).

46. Le Corbusier's Unité de Habitation was designed for 1600 inhabitants in 360 units.

47. On the communal body or *dom-kommuna*, see Kopp, *Town and Revolution*, passim, especially pp. 144–55.

48. Figs. 31–55 are from *SA*, 1930, No. 1-2. They are illustrations of Ginzburg's and Barshch's "Green City" project for the decentral-

ization of Moscow and a linear decentralist project for Magnitogorsk by Barshch, Okhitovich, and others.

49. Figure 36 has been inverted. See Ceccarelli, Fig. 21.

50. Figure 37 is actually only a portion of the complete rendering. See Kopp, *Town and Revolution*, Fig. 154.

51. Figure 38 is a detail of Fig. 52; it represents a station with its attendant communal facilities, i.e., "communal body."

52. Figure 48 is an inverted detail of Fig. 52.

53. On the function of clubs in the USSR at this time see El Lissitzky, *Russia*, pp. 43–45, and Kopp, *Town and Revolution*, pp. 116–26.

54. Figures 56–61 are actually from I. I. Leonidov's project of 1930 for Magnitogorsk (published in *SA*, V, 1930, No. 3). See Introduction, p. 23, and note 29 above.

55. The structures at the right in Fig. 59 are similar to Leonidov's "Clubs of a new social type" of the previous year. See Kopp, *Town and Revolution*, Figs. 103, 104.

56. The Russian text erroneously cites Figs. 20–23 and 72–76.

57. This building was also ridiculed by being compared with a medieval castle in an anonymous article attacking the continued use of pre-Revolutionary styles in *SA*, II, 1927, No. 2, pp. 47–50. It resembles superficially Vignola's Villa Farnese at Caprarola of 1547–59.

58. The fanciful frames around illustrations 73–75 are typical pseudo-folkish vignettes which were popular in Russian typography in the late 1880s and 1890s. Their use here is purely ironic.

59. In the Russian text, *na Tverskoi*. With *Ulitsa* understood as following, Miliutin is saying "on Tver Street," now Gor'kii St. From the fourteenth century Muscovites called the road to Tver *Tverskaia Ulitsa*, and it was so called when the academician I. I. Rerberg designed the ponderous Central Telegraph and Post Office (between Belinskii and Ogareva Streets) in 1927. Rerberg,

a well-known eclectic before 1917, designed in 1914 the Kiev Station in Moscow which incorporates all manner of styles—including a downstairs waiting room which has columns tapered in the Minoan fashion. The Telegraph building caused great controversy even before it went up; *SA* took up the cudgels against its design in its first issue, in 1926.

60. I. V. Zholtovskii (See Introduction, note 9) was a favorite target of the Soviet modernists because of his unrelenting eclecticism. (The term "academician" was not derogatory, however, but merely identified him as a member of the Academy.) Zholtovskii's position is admirably summarized by Kopp in *Town and Revolution*, p. 222, note 27. The Gosbank (State Bank) at No. 12 Neglinnaia Street was originally built by K. Bykovskii in the 1890s in a "Late Renaissance" style (see M. A. Il'in, *Moskva*, 1963). Zholtovskii redesigned the building in 1927 in an "Early Renaissance" style, and major reconstruction took place at the time.

61. In the project for Magnitogorsk that was published in *SA*, 1930, No. 1-2, by Barshch, Okhitovich, and others—from which Miliutin drew for some of his illustrations—a great deal was made of these blocks (invented by the engineer Nekrasov) and of their preparation. Being made of sand, lime, and fibrous organic matter and unkilned, they had good insulating properties, were light in weight, and could be inexpensively manufactured locally. The discussion is reprinted in Ceccarelli, 1970, pp. 218ff.

62. This is a preliminary design for Domnarkomfin by Ginzburg and G. A. Zundblat. It was reproduced in Ginzburg's *Zhilishche* (*Housing*) of 1934 (Fig. 132, p. 107) where it formed part of a considerable promotion (pp. 81–119) of the building, there called the "second apartment house for SNK," i.e., for the Supreme Soviet (see Glossary).

63. By Walter Gropius, Dessau, 1925.

64. The usual English translation from the

German reads quite differently: ''With me, on the contrary, the ideal is nothing else than the material world reflected by the human mind and translated into forms of thought.''

65. Second project for a glass skyscraper, c. 1921.

66. Bernau School, 1929–30, by Hannes Meyer; drawing done by Paul Klee while he was on the Bauhaus faculty, and these four renderings were published in *SA*, III, 1928, No. 5, pp. 149–152. Meyer replaced Gropius as director of the Bauhaus and served from 1928–30. After that time he worked in brigades in the Soviet Union, and his dispatches, lectures, and recollections form some of our most valuable documentation of the period; we have cited one of these in our Introduction, and both Kopp's *Town and Revolution* and the augmented MIT Press edition of El Lissitzky's *Russland* reprint pieces by Meyer. The attribution of Fig. 79 to Klee is by Gustav Platz in the second edition of *Die Baukunst der neuesten Zeit*, Berlin, 1930, p. 95; we have been unable to verify this.

67. Figs. 83–85 are of the Pavillion de l'Esprit Nouveau, at the Paris Exposition of Decorative Arts of 1925.

68. Figs. 86–88 are from the Cook House in Boulogne, 1926.

69. This is the Church House at Ville d'Avray, a sitting room with bar and library.

70. This is Le Corbusier's 1927 project for the League of Nations headquarters in Geneva. Miliutin's caution about giving its correct name probably reflects the distrust the USSR had for the League; it did not join until 1934.

71. All-Union Central Council of Trade Unions. Le Corbusier was disillusioned with the subsequent modifications to his design. His Soviet collaborator, N. Kolli, told Arthur Sprague that the main reason was a shortage of materials, especially glass, but the Stalin period criticized it as bad design. It was to have had a complicated ventilation system consisting of hot or cold air piped between the double glass of its facade;

this was omitted, and the building is unbearably hot in summer, cold in winter. Now the great expanse of green glass is incongruously hung with old-fashioned draperies. The building was further disfigured by enclosing the ground floor, which rendered its pilotis meaningless and created a fenestration that clashes in scale with the rest of the facade. The building was actually finished as the Ministry of Light Industry and since has been converted into a central office for statistical research. It is in generally good condition.

72. Moscow Electrical Engineering Institute, 1929. By V. Movshchan, G. Movshchan, L. Meilman, A. Fisenko, I. Nikolaev, G. Karlsen, under the direction of Professor Kuznetsov. Figs. 93–94 were published in *SA*, IV, 1929, No. 5, p. 170.

73. This chapter is translated into Italian, more or less completely, in Ceccarelli, pp. 131–34.

74. That is, both the ''usual dwellings'' and Miliutin's socialized dwellings. In the following three paragraphs Miliutin concludes that the greatest expense for the collective system (i.e., at 9 m³ per person) would run to about 36 million rubles, which is $\frac{1}{2}$ of the 72 million cited above for the usual dwellings at 9 m³ per person and $\frac{3}{4}$ of the 48 million needed for 6 m³ per person in the usual dwellings.

75. This chapter is also more or less completely translated into Italian in Ceccarelli, pp. 134–39.

76. Again, this is Miliutin's theme and that of the resolution printed in his Appendix 2.

77. Kopp is of the opinion that these demographic studies were undertaken at Miliutin's initiative. (*Town and Revolution*, p. 185).

78. For Sabsovich's heresies, see note 41 above. Larin's position is described in Kopp, *Town and Revolution*, pp. 106–109.

SELECTED BIBLIOGRAPHY

I. Writings of N. A. Miliutin
(Listed Chronologically)

Proekty postanovki sotsial'nogo obespecheniia trudiashchikhsia (*Plans for the setting up of social security for workers*). [Petrograd], 1918–19.

Ed. with V. I. Kamenskii. *Al'bomy chertezhei gospital'noi, kontorskoi mebeli i proektov zdanii uchrezhdenii Tsentrosobesa* (*Albums of sketches of hospital, office furniture and plans of buildings for the establishment of the Central Social Security Department*), Part 1 (Sketches of hospital, office furniture and equipment). Petrograd, Narodnyi Komissariat Truda (People's Commissariat of Labor), 1919.

Po puti k svetlym daliam kommunizma (*On the way to the brilliant works of communism*). Petrograd, Narodnyi Komissariat Truda (People's Commissariat of Labor), 1919.

Rukovodstvo po sostavleniiu otchetov mestnykh sobesov (*Guidance in drawing up accounts for local social security agencies*). Moscow, Nar-

odnyi Komissariat Truda (People's Commissariat of Labor), 1919.

Organizatsiia sotsial'noi vzaimopomoshchi v derevne (*The organization of social mutual aid in the village*). Moscow, Narodnyi Komissariat Sotsial'nego (People's Commissariat of Social Security). 1921.

"Bor'ba za novyi byt i sovetskii urbanizm" ("The struggle for a new mode of life and Soviet urbanism"), in B. Lunin, ed., *Socialist cities . . .*, 1930 [see], pp. 116–119.

Problema stroitel'stva sotsialisticheskikh gorodov: Osnovnye voprosy ratsional'noi planirovki i stroitel'stva naselennykh mest USSR (*The problem of building socialist cities: Basic questions regarding the rational planning and building of settlements in the USSR; "Sotsgorod"*). Moscow and Leningrad, State Publishing House, 1930.

"A new organization of life," "V.O.K.S." (Magazine of the Soviet Union Society for Cultural Relations with Foreign Countries), Moscow, II, 1930, No. 1, pp. 29–31. Brief translation of Chap. 6 of the preceding book.

"Osnovnye voprosy: zhilishchno-bytovogo stroitel'stva SSSR" (Basic questions: the construction of residential living in the SSSR"). *Sovetskaia Arkhitektura*, I, No. 1-2, Jan.-Apr. 1931, pp. 2–4.

"Zapiski o Leonidovshchine" ("Notes on Leonidovism"). *Ibid.*, p. 102.

"Proekt kurortnoi stolovoi klub" ("Project for a resort dining club"). *Ibid.*, II, No. 1, Jan.-Feb. 1932, pp. 53–57.

"Vazhneishie zadachi sovremennogo etapa Sovetskoi arkhitektury." ("Major problems of the present period of Soviet architecture"). *Ibid.* No. 2-3, Mar.-June 1932, pp. 3–9.

"K novomu zakonu o stroitel'stve naselennykh mest" ("Toward a new law on the construction of populated settlements"). *Ibid.*, No. 4, July-Aug. 1932, pp. 3–4.

[Address at the opening of an exhibition of German architecture], (text in Russian and Ger-

man). Ibid., No. 5-6, Sept.-Dec. 1932, pp. 17–18.

"Iasli" ("Nurseries"). *Ibid.*, pp. 81–102.

"Osnovnye voprosy teorii Sovetskoi arkhitektury" ("Basic questions on a theory of Soviet architecture"). *Ibid.*, III, 1933, No. 2, Mar.-Apr., pp. 6–12: No. 3, May-June, pp. 1–16; No. 5, Sept.-Oct., pp. 17–21; No. 6, Nov.-Dec., pp. 2–11.

"Konstruktivizm i funktsionalizm: K kharakteristike arkhitekturnykh techenii XX veka" ("Constructivism and functionalism: Concerning the characteristics of architectural tendencies of the twentieth century"). *Arkhitektura SSSR*, 1935, No. 8, pp. 5–10.

Comments in *Arkhitektura Dvortsa Sovetov: Materialy V Plenum Pravleniia Soiuza Sovetskikh Arkhitektorov, SSSR, 1–4 iiulia 1939 goda* (*Architecture of the Palace of the Soviets: Contributions of the 5th Plenum of the Board of the Union of Soviet Architecture, 1–4 July 1939*), Moscow, Publishing House of the Academy of Architecture, USSR, 1939, pp. 43–44.

II. General Bibliography
(Further specific references are to be found in the Notes)

Afanas'ev, K. N., and V. E. Khazanova. *Iz Istorii Sovetskoi Arkhitektury: 1917–1925* (*From the History of Soviet Architecture: 1917–1925*). Moscow, Academy of Sciences, 1963. A continuation volume for 1926–1932 was published in 1970. See Introduction, note 8.

Arkhitektura. Journal issued by the Moscow Society of Architects (MAO). Two issues only (1923). See Introduction, note 29.

Arkhitektura SSSR. Journal issued by the Union of Soviet Architects. K. Alabian, ed., 1933–36. It is still published.

Blumenfeld, Hans. "Regional and City Planning in the Soviet Union." *Task* (Cambridge, Mass.), No. 3, Oct. 1942.

Bol'shaia Sovetskaia Entsiklopediia (*The Larger Soviet Encyclopedia*). 65 vols. Moscow,

State Publishing House, 1926–47; 2nd ed., 51 vols., 1950–58.

Bourke-White, Margaret. *Eyes on Russia* (with a preface by Maurice Hindus). NYC, Simon and Schuster, 1931.

Bylinkin et al. *Istoriia Sovetskoi Arkhitektury: 1917–1958* (*History of Soviet Architecture: 1917–1958*). Moscow, State Publishing House of Literature on Construction, Architecture, and Construction Materials, 1962.

Ceccarelli, Paolo, ed. *La costruzione della città sovietica 1929–31* (Quaderni di architettura e urbanistica, collana Polis No. 8). Padua, Marsilio Editori, 1970. [Spanish edition: *La construcción de la ciudad soviética* (Colección ciencia urbanística, No. 9), Barcelona, Editorial Gili, 1972.] Among documents included are most of Miliutin's Chaps. 5, 13, and 14; Ginzburg's and Barshch's "Green City"; a piece by Sabsovich; and the resolution of the 1930 Bolshevik Party Congress. See Introduction, note 1.

Chernikhov, Iakov. *Arkhitekturnye Fantazii* (*Architectural Fantasies*). Leningrad, International Books, 1933.

—— *Bazy sovremennoi arkhitektury* (*Bases of contemporary architecture*). Leningrad, Leningrad Society of Architects, 1930.

Collins, George R. "Linear Planning throughout the World." *Journal of the Society of Architectural Historians*, XVIII, Oct. 1959, pp. 74–93.

—— "Linear Planning." *Forum* (Amsterdam), XX, No. 5, Mar. 1968, entire issue.

—— "A Bibliography of Linear Planning." *Newsletter of the Urban History Group* (Milwaukee, Wis.), No. 29, Apr. 1970, pp. 2–12.

—— and Christiane Crasemann Collins. *Camillo Sitte and the Birth of Modern City Planning.* NYC, Random House, 1965.

Conrads, Ulrich, and Hans G. Sperlich. *The Architecture of Fantasy.* Edited, translated, and expanded by Christiane Crasemann Collins and George R. Collins. NYC, Praeger, 1962.

Drabkin, A. D. "American Architects and Engineers in Russia." *Pencil Points*, XI, June 1930, pp. 435–440.

Fariello, Francesco. "L'urbanistica e l'abitazione in Russia." *Architettura*, XV, Sept. 1936, pp. 441–460.

Frampton, Kenneth. "Notes on Soviet Urbanism, 1917–32." *Architects' Year Book*, XII, 1968, pp. 238–252.

Ginzburg, Moisei Iakovlevich. (The following list is only a small selection of his writings.)

—— *Ritm v Arkhitekture* (*Rhythm in Architecture*). Moscow, "Sredi Kollektsionerov" ("Among the Collectivists"), 1923. See Introduction, note 29.

—— *Stil' i Epokha* (*Style and Epoch*). Moscow, State Publishing House, 1924.

—— "Mezhdunarodnyi front sovremennoi arkhitektury" (The international front of contemporary architecture"). *Sovremennaia Arkhitektura (SA)*, I, 1926, No. 2, pp. 41–46.

—— "Itogi i Perspektivy" ("Results and Perspectives"). *SA*, II, 1927, No. 3-4, pp. 112–118.

—— "O Leonidovshchine" ("Concerning Leonidovism"). *SA*, II, 1927, No. 4, p. 116.

—— "Zeitgenössische Architektur in Russland." *Die Baugilde* (Berlin), Oct. 1928, pp. 1370, 1372. Reprinted in El Lissitzky, *Russia*, pp. 155–159.

—— "Zelenyi Gorod" ("The Green City"). *SA*, V, No. 1-2 (1930), pp. 23–27.

—— "Perepiska s Lekorbuz'e" ("Correspondence with Le Corbusier"). *Ibid.*, p. 61.

—— *Zhilishche* (*Housing*). Moscow, Gosstroiizdat, 1934.

—— "Tvorcheskie Otcheti" ("Creative Reports"). *Arkhitektura SSSR*, No. 5, 1935, pp. 6ff.

—— "Mass Production Housing Proposals in the USSR." Translated from the Russian by W. G. Cass, *Architectural Association Journal*, LIX, No. 6, Nov.-Dec. 1944, pp. 114–116.

Gornyi, S. See Svetlov, F. and Introduction, notes 65, 68.

Grabar', I. E., ed. *Istoriia Russkogo Iskusstva* (*History of Russian Art*). 13 vols. Moscow, Academy of Sciences, Vol. XI, 1957. See Introduction, note 6.

Gray, Camilla. *The Great Experiment: Russian Art, 1917–1922.* London, Thames and Hudson, 1962. Reissued in small format, NYC, Abrams, 1970.

Hamilton, George Heard. *Art and Architecture of Russia.* Baltimore, Pelican Books, 1954.

Hruška, Emmanuel. *Rasvitie Gradostroitel'stva* (*The Development of City Building*). Russian translation of a Czechoslovakian text by Ladislav Gornish and wife. Bratislava, Czechoslovakia, Academy of Sciences, 1963. See Introduction, note 6.

Il'in, M. "Modern architecture in the Soviet Union." "*V.O.K.S.*", I, No. 8-10, Aug.-Oct. 1930, pp. 51–55.

Il'in, Mikhail Andreevich. *Moskva* (*Moscow*). Moscow, "Iskusstvo" ("Art"), 1963.

—— *Vesniny* (*The Vesnins*). Moscow, Academy of Sciences, 1960.

Il'in, M. (pseud. for Il'in Iakolovich Marshak). *Rasskaz o Velekom Plane* (Story of the Great Plan). Moscow and Leningrad, State Publishing House, 1930. Translated as *New Russia's Primer: the Story of the Five Year Plan.* Cambridge, Mass., Houghton Mifflin, 1931, by George S. Counts and Nucia P. Lodge. Published in Britain as *Moscow has a Plan; a Soviet Primer.* Jonathan Cape, London, 1931. Reprinted in English as *The Story of the Five Year Plan* (with 65-page vocabulary for Russian schoolchildren). Moscow, Co-operative Publishing Society of Foreign Workers in the USSR, 1932. See Introduction Note 5 regarding these publications.

Kaganovich, L. M. *Socialist Reconstruction of Moscow and Other Cities in the USSR.* No translator given. NYC, International Publishers, 1931. Extracts printed in "*V.O.K.S.*", III, No.

5-6, May-June 1932, pp. 135–150.

Kampfmeyer, Hans. "Town Planning in Soviet Russia," *Bauen und Wohnen*, IV, No. 1-2, 1932, pp. 9–38. Includes a summary of Miliutin's book.

Kaufman, E. C. "Housing and Territorial Planning in Russia." *Architecture and Building News*, CXLIV, Dec. 1935, pp. 382–384.

Khan-Magomedov, S. O. "Ivan Leonidov: 1902–1960." *Arkhitektura SSSR*, No. 16, 1964, pp. 103–116.

Khiger, R. *Puti arkhitekturnoi mysli 1917–1932. (Ways of architectural thinking 1917–1932)*, Moscow, Ogiz-Izogiz, 1933.

—— "M. Ia. Ginzburg." *Sovetskaia Arkhitektura*, No. 15, 1963, pp. 117–136.

Kopp, Anatole. *Ville et Revolution*. Paris, Editions Anthropos, 1967. English translation by Thomas E. Burton, *Town and Revolution: Soviet Architecture and City Planning 1917–1935*. NYC, Braziller, 1970. Excerpts from Miliutin's Chap. 6 are included as Appendix III.

Le Corbusier [Charles Edouard Jeanneret]. *La Ville Radieuse*. Paris, Editions d'Architecture d'Aujourd'hui, 1935. English edition, *The Radiant City*. NYC, Orion Press, 1967. See Introduction, note 2.

Lissitzky, El. *Russland. Die Rekonstruktion der Architektur in der Sowjetunion* (Neues Bauen in der Welt, Vol. 1). Vienna, Verlag Anton Schroll, 1930. Reprinted as *1929: Russland: Architektur für eine Weltrevolution*. Berlin, Frankfort, Vienna, Ullstein Bauwelt Fundamente, No. 14 (Ulrich Conrads, ed.), 1965, with extensive appendixes containing documents of the time. English translation by Eric Dluhosch, *Russia: An Architecture for World Revolution*. Cambridge, Mass., MIT Press, 1970.

Lubetkin, Berthold. "Recent Developments of Town Planning in the USSR." *Architectural Review*, LXXXI, No. 426, May 1932, pp. 209–214.

—— "Town and Landscape Planning in Soviet Russia." *Architectural Association Journal*, XLVIII, Jan. 1933, p. 186. Summarized in

Journal of the Town Planning Institute, XIX, Feb. 1933, pp. 69–75.

—— "Soviet Architecture; Notes on Development from 1917–1932." *Architectural Association Journal*, LXXXI, No. 802, May 1956, pp. 260–264; No. 805, Sept.-Oct. 1956, pp. 85–89.

Lunin, B., ed. *Goroda sotsializma i sotsialisticheskaia rekonstruktsiia byta (Socialist cities and socialist reconstruction of the mode of living)*. [Moscow], Rabotnik Prosveshcheniia (The Worker of Enlightenment), 1930. Collection of articles by A. Goltsman, V. Zelenko, N. Krupskaia, A. Lunacharskii, N. Miliutin, L. Sabsovich, A. Epshtein, and others.

Martens, Boris. "Das Problem des sozialistischen Städtebaues." *Die Form* (Berlin), No. 5, 15 May 1932, pp. 49–52. Excellent short summary of Miliutin's text.

Matsa, I. L. *Sovetskoe Iskusstvo za 15 Let (Fifteen Years of Soviet Art)*. Moscow, State Publishing House, 1933.

May, Ernst. "From Frankfurt to the New Russia." *Frankfurter Zeitung*, No. 892, 30 Nov. 1930. Reprinted in El Lissitzky, *Russia*, pp. 175–179.

—— "Der Bau der Städte in der UdSSR," *Das Neue Frankfurt*, V, No. 7, 1931. This was a famous lecture delivered in connection with CIAM affairs in Berlin on 6 June 1931; May was introduced by the architects Victor Bourgeois, Cornell van Eesteren, and Walter Gropius. A summary appeared in *Bauwelt* (Berlin), XXII, No. 24, 11 June 1931, pp. 817–818 and was reprinted in *La cité* (Brussels), IX, No. 11, July 1931, pp. 229–231. The full text was reprinted in *Das Neue Russland*, Nos. 8/9, 1931, and in *Tekhne* (Brussels) V, n.s., No. 5, Jan. 1932, pp. 77–84, with illustrations in its companion periodical *La cité*, X, No. 5, Jan. 1932, pp. 65–78, and has also been reprinted in El Lissitzky, *Russia*, pp. 188–203.

—— "Cities of the Future," *Survey* (London), No. 38, 1961, pp. 179–186.

Meyer, Hannes. See Schmidt, Hans, below.

Minervin, G. B., ed. *Magnitogorsk*. Moscow, State Publishing House of Literature on Construction, Architecture, and Construction Materials, 1961.

Nevins, Allan, and Frank Ernest Hill. *Ford, Expansion and Challenge, 1915–1933*. N.Y., Charles Scribner's Sons, 1937, Appendix I, "The Russian Adventures," (pp. 673–84).

Ostrowski, Waclaw. *Contemporary town planning: From the origins to the Athens Charter*. Transl. by Krystyna Keplicz. The Hague, International Federation for Housing and Planning. Chap. 9.

Parkins, Maurice Frank. *Town Planning in Soviet Russia*. Chicago, University of Chicago Press, 1953. See Introduction, note 6.

Pasternak, A. "U.R.S.S.: les problèmes de l'édification des villes socialistes en U.R.S.S." *Architecture d'Aujourd'hui*, 1931, No. 8, pp. 5–9.

Quilici, Vieri. *L'architettura del costruttivismo*. Bari, Editori Laterza, 1969. Reprints of documents of the period.

Sabsovich, Leonard Moiseevich, *Sotsialisticheskie Goroda (Socialist Cities)*. Moscow, State Technical Publishing House, 1930.

—— *SSSR cherez 10 Let (The USSR in Ten Years)*. Moscow, The Moscow Worker, 1930.

Schapiro, Leonard. *The Communist Party of the Soviet Union*. NYC, Random House, 1960.

Schmidt, Hans, and Hannes Meyer. *Schweizer Staedtebauer bei den Sowjets*, Basel, Genossenschafts-Buchdruckerei [1932].

Shvidkovsky, Oleg A., ed. *Building in the USSR 1917–1932*. NYC, Praeger, 1971. This, by a number of Russian authors, is a reprint of a special issue of *Architectural Design* for Feb. 1970.

Sovetskaia Arkhitektura (Soviet Architecture). Journal issued by the Commissariat of Education (Narkompros), 1931–34. Edited by N. A. Miliutin.

Sovremennaia Arkhitektura (Contemporary

Architecture, SA). Journal issued by the Union of Contemporary Architects (OSA). Edited by M. Ia. Ginzburg and A. Vesnin (1926–1930).

Sprague, Arthur. "Chernikhov and Constructivism," *Survey* (London), No. 38, 1961, pp. 69–77.

—— "N. A. Miliutin and Linear Planning in the USSR." Unpublished Master's Essay in the Department of Art History and Archaeology, Columbia University, 1967.

Starr, S. Frederick. "Writings from the 1960s on the Modern Movement in Russia." *Journal of the Society of Architectural Historians*, XXX, No. 2, May 1971, pp. 170–178.

Sushkevich, I. G. *Planirovka i Stroitel'stvo Gorodov SSSR* (*Planning and Building of Cities of the USSR*). Moscow, Publishing House of All-Union Academies, 1939. See Introduction, note 6.

Sutton, Antony C. *Western Technology and Soviet Economic Development*, I (1917–1930), II (1930–1945), Stanford University, 1968, 1971.

Svetlov, F., and S. Gornyi. "Sotsialisticheskii gorod v besklassovom obshchestve" ("The socialist city in a society without classes").

Planovoe khoziaistvo, No. 7, 1934. Reprinted in Italian in Ceccarelli, 1970, pp. 168–187.

Tafuri, Manfredo. "Les premières hypothèses de planification urbaine dans la Russie soviétique 1918–1925." *Archithese* (Zurich), No. 7, 1973, pp. 34–41.

—— et al. *Socialismo, città, architettura URSS 1917–1937; il contributo degli architetti europei* (Collana di Architettura, 3). Rome, Officina Edizioni, 1971.

Willen, Paul Larner. "Soviet Architecture in Transformation: a Study in Ideological Manipulation." Unpublished Master's Essay in the Department of History, Columbia University, NYC, 1953. A very brief synopsis, hardly useful for our purposes appeared in *Problems of Communism*, II, No. 6, 1953, pp. 24–33.

Zitte, Kamillo. *Gorodskoe stroitel'stvo s tochki zreniia ego khudozhestvennykh printsipov* (*City Planning according to its Artistic Principles*). Edited and with Preface by P. A. Mamatov. Translated from the fifth German edition, by I. I. Vul'fert. Moscow, Printing Office of the Moscow Guberniia [District] Engineer, 1925. See Introduction, note 24.

WE ARE INDEBTED TO PROF. S. FREDERICK STARR FOR CHECKING THIS GLOSSARY — G.R.C.

GLOSSARY

Agrogoroda (pl.): Agricultural cities. These were planned as counterparts to industrial cities in the program of breaking down distinctions between city and country.

Artel: A traditional Russian cooperative association of workers banded together for various types of production.

ASNOVA: Assotsiatsiia Novykh Arkhitektorov. Association of New Architects. Organized by Professor Ladovskii and others in 1923.

Dom-kommuna: Communal house. "... an urban element functioning as a small autonomous commune in relation to a whole series of services and bodies." (Kopp, *Town and Revolution*, p. 130)

Fermy (pl.): Farms.

FUBR: Fond Uluchsheniia Byta Rabochikh i Sluzhashchikh. Fund for the Amelioration of the (living) Conditions of Workers and Employees.

Glz: Gosudarstvennoe Izdatel'stvo. State Publishing House.

Glavlit: Glavnoe Upravlenie po Delam Literatury i Izdatel'stv. Main Directorate of Literature and Publishing Houses.

Gosbank: Gosudarstvennyi Bank. State Bank.

Gosplan: Gosudarstvennyi Komitet Planirovaniia SSR. State Planning Commission. Highest planning body of the USSR.

Kolkhoz: Kollektivnoe Khoziaistvo. Collective farm.

Kombinat: An industrial or agricultural combine composed of a number of productive units, or a dwelling combination of living cells and common facilities.

MAO: Moskovskoe Arkhitekturnoe Obshchestvo. Moscow Architectural Society. Pre-Revolutionary organization, reactivated in the 1920s.

Narkompros: Narodnyi Komissariat Prosveshcheniia. People's [or Public] Commissariat of Public Education. Founded 1918. Headed by A. V. Lunacharskii until 1929. Miliutin was attached to the Communist Academy which was under it.

Narkomtrud: Narodnyi Komissariat Truda. People's Commissariat of Labor.

Narkomzdrav: Narodnyi Komissariat Zdravo-okhraneniia. People's Commissariat of Public Health.

Narpit: Narodnoe Pitanie. People's Food Commissariat.

NK RKI (Narkomrabkrin): Narodnyi Komissariat Raboche-Krest'ianskoi Inspektsii. People's Commissariat of Workers' and Peasants' Inspectorates.

Ogoroda: Family garden allotments.

OSA: Ob'edinenie Sovremennykh Arkhitektorov. The Union of Contemporary Architects. Founded in 1925 by M. Ia. Ginzburg and the Vesnin brothers, it was the core of the Constructivist movement. Published *SA* (*Sovremennaia Arkhitektura*) [see]. "Osa" means "wasp" in Russian.

RSFSR: Rossiiskaia Sovetskaia Federativnaia Sotsialisticheskaia Respublika. Russian Soviet Federated Socialist Republic. Largest and wealthiest of the 15 republics of which the Soviet Union is composed; it is ethnographically the Great Russian nation, plus Siberia.

SA: 1. *Sovremennaia Arkhitektura* (Contemporary Architecture). Journal of OSA, published 1926–30. Edited by M. Ia. Ginzburg and A. Vesnin. 2. *Sovetskaia Arkhitektura* (Soviet Architecture). Journal issued by Narkompros, published 1931–34. Edited by N. A. Miliutin.

SASS: Sektor Arkhitektorov Sotsialisticheskogo Stroitelistva. Architects' Association for Socialist Construction. A regrouping of OSA in 1931. It was soon merged into the new Union of Soviet Architects.

SNK: Sovet Narodnykh Komissarov (Sovnarkom). The Council of People's Commissars. Its decrees represented the supreme law of the Soviet Union.

Sotsgorod: Sotsialisticheskii Gorod (Socialist City). This is the title by which Miliutin's book is generally known; it was, however, commonly used to refer to any town organized along new socialist principles.

Sovkhoz: Sovetskoe Khoziaistvo. Farm owned and managed by the State.

Stroikom: Stroitel'nyi Komitet. Construction Committee [of the RSFSR]. Headed by M. Ia. Ginzburg.

TsSU: Tsentral'noe Statisticheskoe Upravlenie. Central Statistical Directorate.

TsK VKP(b): Tsentral'nyi Komitet Vsesoiuznaia Kommunisticheskaia Partiia/Bol'shevikov. Central Committee of the Bolshevik Communist Party.

V.O.K.S.: Vsesoiuznoe Obshchestvo Kul'turnoi Sviazi s Zagranitsei. Soviet Union Society for Cultural Relations with Foreign Countries. From Jan. 1931 to Oct. 1934 published in several languages an informative propaganda magazine called *"V.O.K.S."* (Resumed publication in late 1930s.)

VOPRA: Vsesoiuznoe Obshchestvo Proletarskikh Arkhitektorov. The All-Union Society of Proletarian Architects. Organized in 1929 as part of the general proletarian movement in the arts.

VSNKh: Vysshii Sovet Narodnogo Khoziaistva. Supreme Council on the National Economy.

VTsSPS: Vsesoiuznyi Tsentral'nyi Sovet Professional'nykh Soiuzov (Tsentrosoiuz). The All-Union Central Council of Trade Unions. This is the entity for which Le Corbusier designed the office building in Moscow.

●

DATE DUE

FEB 2 2 1982			
MAR 2 9 1983			
30 505 JOSTEN'S			